The Tyndale New Testament Commentaries

General Editor: Professor R. V. G. Tasker, M.A., B.D.

THE EPISTLE TO
THE HEBREWS

THE EPISTLE TO THE

HEBREWS

AN INTRODUCTION AND COMMENTARY

by

THOMAS HEWITT, B.D., M.TH.

Wm. B. Eerdmans Publishing Company
Grand Rapids, Michigan

First Edition, November 1960
Eighth printing, February 1978

Library of Congress Catalog Card Number: 61-8379
ISBN 0-8028-1414-X

PHOTOLITHOPRINTED BY EERDMANS PRINTING COMPANY
GRAND RAPIDS, MICHIGAN, UNITED STATES OF AMERICA

GENERAL PREFACE

ALL who are interested in the teaching and study of the New Testament today cannot fail to be concerned with the lack of commentaries which avoid the extremes of being unduly technical or unhelpfully brief. It is the hope of the editor and publishers that this present series will do something towards the supply of this deficiency. Their aim is to place in the hands of students and serious readers of the New Testament, at a moderate cost, commentaries by a number of scholars who, while they are free to make their own individual contributions, are united in a common desire to promote a truly biblical theology.

The commentaries are primarily exegetical and only secondarily homiletic, though it is hoped that both student and preacher will find them informative and suggestive. Critical questions are fully considered in introductory sections, and also, at the author's discretion, in additional notes.

The commentaries are based on the Authorized (King James) Version, partly because this is the version which most Bible readers possess, and partly because it is easier for commentators, working on this foundation, to show why, on textual and linguistic grounds, the later versions are so often to be preferred. No one translation is regarded as infallible, and no single Greek manuscript or group of manuscripts is regarded as always right! Greek words are transliterated to help those unfamiliar with the language, and to save those who do know Greek the trouble of discovering what word is being discussed.

There are many signs today of a renewed interest in what the

5

Bible has to say and of a more general desire to understand its meaning as fully and clearly as possible. It is the hope of all those concerned with this series that God will graciously use what they have written to further this end.

R. V. G. Tasker.

CONTENTS

AUTHOR'S PREFACE

THE Epistle to the Hebrews is, perhaps, the most theological book in the New Testament. Christology, soteriology and eschatology play an important part in this work, while the doctrine of man, though not quite so prominent, is certainly not absent. There are only two brief references, however, to the Church and one of these is a quotation from the Old Testament. This may account for the total absence of any reference to the sacrament of the Lord's Supper.

There are a number of passages which are extremely difficult to elucidate, and this may be the reason for its lack of popularity in some quarters, but none of these difficulties has been consciously avoided in this verse-by-verse commentary. Many works have been consulted but the three commentaries which have been my constant companions and from which I have received the most help are William Manson's, Westcott's and Moffatt's. It may be true to say that Manson's work is not a commentary in the true sense of the term, nor am I aware that it makes such a claim, but it is amazing how much is covered in that excellent book. I have always been reluctant to disagree with these three delightful companions but there have been occasions when I have felt bound to do so.

This Epistle is set apart from all other books in the New Testament by its reference to the priesthood of Christ. The importance and necessity of this aspect of Christ's life can never be exaggerated, and how much poorer the New Testament would have been without any reference to Christ's priesthood! Indeed it would not be untrue to say that the New Testament would not have been complete without this important subject.

For many years I have been dissatisfied with the traditional interpretation of Christ's agony in the garden. There seem to be, from my point of view, too many apparent contradictions, and sometimes I have felt that the honour of Christ has been challenged. In chapter v. 7 I have suggested another approach with the sincere hope that this important and sacred subject may receive further examination.

THOMAS HEWITT.

CHIEF ABBREVIATIONS

AV	English Authorized Version (King James).
RV	English Revised Version, 1881.
RSV	American Revised Standard Version, 1946.
LXX	Septuagint Version.
Arndt and Gingrich	*A Greek-English Lexicon of the New Testament* by William F. Arndt and F. Wilbur Gingrich, 1957.
Bruce	*The Epistle to the Hebrews* by A. B. Bruce.
Calvin	*Commentary on the Hebrews* by John Calvin, translated by John Owen, 1853.
Knox	*The New Testament of our Lord and Saviour Jesus Christ* by R. A. Knox, 1945.
Leonard	*The Authorship of the Epistle to the Hebrews* by William Leonard, 1939.
Moulton and Howard	*A Grammar of New Testament Greek*, Vol. II, by James Hope Moulton and Wilbert Francis Howard, 1929.
Manson	*The Epistle to the Hebrews* by William Manson, 1957.
Moffatt	*The Epistle to the Hebrews* (The International Critical Commentaries) by James Moffatt, 1924.
Moule	*An Idiom-book of New Testament Greek* by C. F. D. Moule, 1953.

Moulton	*A Grammar of New Testament Greek*, Vol. I, by J. H. Moulton, 3rd edition, reprinted 1949.
MM	*The Vocabulary of the Greek New Testament* by James Hope Moulton and George Milligan, 1949.
Nairne	*The Epistle of Priesthood* by Alexander Nairne, 1913.
Owen	*The Epistle to the Hebrews* by John Owen, 1839.
Rendall	*Epistle to the Hebrews* by Frederic Rendall, 1883.
Tasker	*The Gospel in the Epistle to the Hebrews* by R. V. G. Tasker, 2nd edition, 1956.
Vaughan	*The Epistle to the Hebrews* by C. J. Vaughan, 1890.
Westcott	*The Epistle to the Hebrews* by Brooke Foss Westcott, 1892.
Wickham	*The Epistle to the Hebrews* (Westminster Commentaries) by E. C. Wickham, 1922.
Zuntz	*The Text of the Epistles* by G. Zuntz, 1953.

ACKNOWLEDGEMENT

Scripture quotations from the Revised Standard Version (copyrighted 1946 and 1952 by the Division of Christian Education, National Council of Churches, U.S.A.) are used by permission.

INTRODUCTION

THE author of this great work never mentions his name, nor is there any direct evidence within the Epistle which helps us definitely to identify him. It is true that external evidence eventually associates the name of Paul with the Epistle, yet even here the evidence is not free from doubts. Like the strange and mysterious figure of Melchisedec, who suddenly appeared on the stage of human history, and just as suddenly disappeared, yet through a single act became immortalized, so the author of Hebrews through the production of this magnificent Epistle lives on for ever. But who he was, and to whom he addressed the Epistle, and the destination to which it was originally sent, are problems unlikely to be solved from the data at our disposal at present.

We are told that one of the assured results of modern scholarship is that Paul was not the author of the Epistle. This negative conclusion does not help us to find the name of the true author, but it challenges the traditional assertion of Pauline authorship, and leaves the field wide open for discussion.

For convenience we may consider the history of opinion about the authorship under three headings: the evidence from the West; the evidence from the East; and the attitude of the Church from the time of the Reformation.

a. *Evidence from the West*

It is generally agreed that the various texts found in the most important New Testament MSS arose within important Christian centres. From these MSS we can obtain some idea of the books which were recognized as canonical, and those which were considered doubtful, at the various centres from which the MSS came. The so-called Western text, so far as one can tell, does not appear to have received Hebrews into the Canon earlier than the third century; and even when it did, the Epistle was placed at the end of the Pauline Epistles, revealing the uncertainty of the Western Church. Yet the evidence at our disposal shows quite clearly that Hebrews was known in the West from early times, especially in Rome. Clement of Rome quoted some of its phrases from memory and used some of its actual words in his Epistle to the Corinthian Church written in AD 96. There is also some evidence that it was known to the author of the *Shepherd of Hermas* and Justin Martyr, both of whom had contact with Rome. Yet it was in the West and at Rome that both the Pauline authorship and the canonicity of the Epistle were challenged. The Muratorian Canon, which is generally held to be the Canon which had obtained authority in Rome towards the end of the second century, not only negatively excludes Hebrews from canonicity, but also formally excludes it from the Pauline catalogue.

This rejection of both its canonicity and apostolicity by the Church of Rome in the second century is one of the reasons put forward for the rejection of the Pauline authorship today. On the other hand, it might be argued that, as the Church of Rome was wrong about its canonicity, it may have been equally wrong about its apostolicity. Furthermore, if the Epistle, as some suggest, was first sent to the East and only later reached Rome, it would have been quite natural for that Church to look upon a supposed anonymous letter, so unlike the genuine Pauline letters, as not being by the hand of the apostle.

A tradition exists which asserts that Hippolytus of Rome and his master, Irenaeus of Lyons, said that the Epistle to the Hebrews was not Paul's. In the North African Church similar doubts are evident. Tertullian in his opposition to the edict of forgiveness of Maximus quotes Hebrews vi. 4–8, and ascribes it to Barnabas. He thus clearly regarded the letter as un-Pauline, and it is possible that he also denied its canonicity.

b. *Evidence from the East*

The Eastern Church's viewpoint concerning the canonicity of
the Epistle is expressed by its position before the Pastoral
Epistles in the two important MSS Vaticanus and Sinaiticus.
The Chester Beatty papyrus, which has affinities with the
East and which dates from the early part of the third century,
places Hebrews after Romans as the second Epistle in the
Corpus Paulinum. These MSS most probably express the views of
the great Alexandrian scholars. Towards the end of the second
century, or at the beginning of the third, Clement of Alexandria, according to Eusebius, in his work *Hypotyposes* mentioned that the Epistle to the Hebrews was Paul's, but that, as
it was destined for Jews, it was written in the Hebrew language,
and Luke translated it with zealous care and published it for
the Greeks. Eusebius also mentions that Clement maintained
that the blessed presbyter (most probably Pantaenus) stated
that the reason for the omission of the usual epistolary address
was the fact that the Lord Himself was the Apostle to the
Hebrews whereas Paul was the apostle to the Gentiles.[1]

As there is no evidence that the Alexandrian scholars as a
whole held the view of a Hebrew original, it is highly probable
that Clement himself invented the theory to explain the difference of style between this Epistle and those accepted as Paul's.

We know that Origen, who succeeded Clement of Alexandria as the leading scholar of his day in Alexandria, could
not accept the view of his predecessor that the Epistle, as he
knew it, was a Greek translation from a Hebrew original. From
the last Homilies of Origen Eusebius records a statement that
the elegance of the Epistle does not harmonize with the self-
confessed inelegance of St. Paul's speech (2 Cor. xi. 6). From
this Origen drew the following conclusion—the thoughts are
Paul's, but the phraseology and composition belong to
another, who recorded the apostle's thoughts and, as it were,
produced a scholarly reproduction of what his master said.

[1] Eusebius, *H.E.*, vi. 14; also *H.E.*, v. 11; cf. vi. 13.

Who this recorder was 'God alone knows'. It seems that Origen knew that there were two suggestions concerning the redactor. One assigned the Epistle to Luke, and the other to Clement of Rome.[1] One important sentence of Origen reads as follows: 'If any church, therefore, holds that this Epistle is of Paul let it have full approval on that matter for it was not without reason that the ancients, or men of old time (*hoi archaioi andres*), passed it on as a letter of Paul's . . .'[2] It appears from this that Origen accepted the Epistle because the tradition of the Eastern fathers at least was behind it.

Little by little the whole Church came to accept the decision of the Eastern Church and regarded Hebrews as Pauline and, therefore, canonical. Yet tradition maintained the distinction between the substance of the writing and its linguistic form; the latter was attributed to a hand other than Paul's.

The mediaeval fathers seem to have supported the idea of a Hebrew original from the hand of Paul, but at the time of the Reformation scholars leaned towards the theory of Origen, which eventually led to the rejection of the Pauline authorship.

c. *Attitude of the Church from the Reformation era*

Luther's doubts about the Pauline authorship were not confined to Protestants, for Cardinal Cajetan rejected both the Pauline authorship and the canonicity of Hebrews. Erasmus rejected the Pauline authorship but seems to have accepted the decision of the Church about its canonicity.

Luther's rejection of the Pauline authorship was followed by Melanchthon, Osiander, Calvin, Beza and others. Yet it was stoutly defended by Flacius Illyricus, and also by the Roman Catholic scholars, Estius and Bellarmine, and this position seems to have held sway until the nineteenth century, when many Protestant scholars rejected the Pauline authorship completely.

F. B. Clogg has summarized the main points which are supposed to be decisive against the Pauline authorship. 'The style

[1] Eusebius, *H.E.*, vi. 14, 2–3.   [2] Eusebius, *H.E.*, vi. 25.

and vocabulary,' he says, 'the attitude to the law, the conception of faith and the High Priesthood of our Lord are not Pauline. Moreover the writer claims that he and his readers have received their knowledge of the Gospel from those who heard the Lord. Paul was emphatic that he received his Gospel from no man.' To this may be added its Alexandrian connection.[1]

Style and vocabulary certainly stand as serious objections to the Pauline authorship, as both Clement of Alexandria and Origen were well aware. Paul's Epistles reveal the missionary and enthusiast rather than the classical scholar, while Hebrews has the touch of the classicist. 'Familiarity with some of the masters of the classical syntax', say MM, 'may be traced in the exact significance of the tenses, in the full and more skilful use of participles and conjunctions, and in the more complex structure of the sentence as compared with the other New Testament writings.' Westcott also draws attention to this when he says, 'It would be difficult to find anywhere passages more exact and poignant in expression than i. 4, ii. 14–18, vii. 26–28, xii. 18–24. The language, the ardour, the rhythm, the parenthetical involutions all contribute to the fact that the writer was a classical scholar.'

These statements do not necessarily mean that Paul *could* not have been the author, but they do show clearly that the usual style of Paul is very different from that of the writer of our Epistle. Yet style and vocabulary should never be the decisive factor in settling questions of authorship. The Pauline authorship of Ephesians, Colossians and the Pastoral Epistles has also been questioned on the ground of style and vocabulary, although modern scholarship is, perhaps, more in favour of Pauline authorship of these Epistles than it was fifty years ago.

Leonard deals very extensively with the peculiarities of vocabulary in Hebrews and shows that this difficulty is highly exaggerated. He also maintains that no other personal

---

[1] *An Introduction to the New Testament*, 1937, p. 135.

vocabulary that is known to us, not only in Christian literature but in the whole range of Hellenistic literature, coincides so much with the vocabulary of Paul as do the 990 words which make up the lexicon of the Epistle to the Hebrews.

Another factor which must be borne in mind is the similarity in style of chapter xiii and the writings of Paul. So close is this that some scholars have suggested that Paul added this chapter to the letter, or that it is a fragment from a Pauline Epistle. Yet there is not the slightest hint anywhere that this chapter was not a part of the original Epistle, nor is there any suggestion that it was added by another hand. But if it is a genuine part of the original letter, and is in harmony with the style of Paul, then it certainly suggests that Paul at least played some part in the composition of this Epistle. On the other hand, it may be that the general exhortations it contains were a characteristic feature of Christian correspondence at the time.

The second main doubt concerning Pauline authorship is theological. For Paul the law was a moral code which could reveal sin, and also, because of the weakness of the flesh, increase its power. The author of Hebrews looks upon the law as a sacerdotal code, whose weakness is inherent in its ritual institutions. In the Pauline letters the law is regarded as a schoolmaster to bring us to Christ; in Hebrews it is a type or figure of the perfect things to come. On the other hand, both Paul and the author of Hebrews speak of the elementary character of the ceremonial law (Gal. iv. 3; Heb. vii. 19), and of Christ as the end of the law (Rom. x. 4; Heb. x. 4–7). Both speak of the old and new covenants, and of the mediatorial work of Christ; and in speaking of the redemptive work of Christ our author appears to be at one with Paul even though he does not attempt to solve the deeper problems as Paul does. Moreover, Tasker may be right when he says, 'Had St. Paul been concerned to develop the contrast between the sacrificial death of Christ and the Levitical system of sacrifice, just as he had in Romans contrasted law and grace, we cannot say that he could not have done so along the lines of this Epistle: and as for the use made in the Epistle of the story of Melchizedek, who can set any limits to the exegetical powers of the converted Jew who had sat at the feet of Gamaliel?'[1]

Although Westcott sees a close connection between the Christology of Hebrews and Paul, he also sees dissimilarity in phraseology. In 2 Corinthians iv. 4 Paul speaks of Christ as 'the image (*eikōn*) of God', and in Colossians i. 15 as 'the image (*eikōn*) of the invisible God'. In Philippians ii. 6, which is dealing with the pre-existence of Christ, our Lord is spoken of as 'being in the form (*morphē*) of God'. In Hebrews those terms do not occur, but the thoughts certainly do, for Christ is the effulgence of God's glory and the very stamp of His nature (i. 3). Westcott further maintains that the Pauline conceptions of Christ as the second Adam and as the Head of the Church do not appear in Hebrews. There can be no doubt that this is correct, but here again the thought is not entirely absent from the Epistle, for Christ as Man is seated at the right hand of God and crowned with glory and honour, all things being put in subjection under His feet (ii. 8), and this is closely related to Ephesians i. 19-23. Also as one similar to and greater than Moses Christ is 'as a son over his own house' (iii. 1-6); as the Captain of their salvation He brings many as sons into glory who are called both His 'brethren' and 'the church' (ii. 10-12); He is also (again like Moses, see Is. lxiii. 11) the 'great shepherd of the sheep' (xiii. 20), i.e. the Head of the Church. Moreover both Paul and the author of Hebrews lay stress upon the divine and human natures of Christ; and both conceive of all things being created through the Son.

A further point to be considered in this connection is the fact that, for Paul, faith is one of the supreme factors in the Christian life. It is the channel through which the grace of salvation enters the life of the believer. Without personal trust, whole-hearted surrender of the believer to Jesus Christ, a man cannot be saved (Eph. ii. 8, 9). Faith is also the ground of our

[1] Tasker, p. 7.

justification (Rom. v. 1). It is not through good works or sound intellectual views that a man is declared righteous by God, but because he is justified by faith apart from works of the law (Rom. iii. 28). Thus for Paul faith is an attitude of the whole man—of his heart, mind and will; and is essentially related to the death of Christ. The writer of Hebrews has only a little to say of this faith. For him faith is primarily concerned with the unseen world of realities and the future. He holds that this world is a copy or shadow of the unseen world, which alone is real and eternal. Men of faith are those who are conscious of this fact and have experienced, even now, the blessings of this other world. It was such faith as this which was the inspiring force in the heroes of the Old Testament (chapter xi).

Furthermore, no exact definition of faith is given in Hebrews; it is simply described as the confidence which makes men certain of what they do not see, and as the proof, or demonstration, of these unseen realities. A. B. Bruce remarks that 'in the Epistle to the Hebrews faith is a force making for personal righteousness and a power helping to make their lives sublime; a faculty of the human mind whereby it can make the future as if it were present'.[1]

The writer of Hebrews does in fact speak of 'justification by faith' and comes very near to St. Paul's thoughts of justifying faith in x. 22 where he speaks of drawing near to God 'in full assurance of faith'. See also xi. 4, 7.

The Alexandrian character of the Epistle and its supposed connections with Philo have led some scholars to deny the Pauline authorship. Philo was the chief representative of the Alexandrian school of pre-Christian Judaism. He is the only Jewish contemporary of our Lord whose writings have come down to us in any considerable quantity. His system was an eclectic one, for he sought to unite Jewish belief with Hellenic culture. Some commentators have gone so far as to say that we cannot understand the Epistle to the Hebrews if we do not

[1] Hastings, *Dictionary of the Bible*, Vol. II, p. 334.

regard it as belonging to the school of Philo, and unless we are conversant with Philo's philosophy. It is maintained that the author's fundamental conception of the antithesis between the passing phenomena and the world of eternal realities was derived from the school of Plato through the writings of Philo. But, though Philo certainly taught that the created things on earth were but a copy of the real and eternal things in heaven, and the author of Hebrews speaks of earthly shadows of heavenly realities, nevertheless, as Gayford rightly points out, 'there are marked differences, and it is doubtful whether more can be proved than the popular influence of Alexandrian Platonism upon the cultured thought of the day'.[1]

It is also claimed that the LXX version used by the author of Hebrews for his Old Testament quotations was the Alexandrian MS, which was also the MS used by Philo. Further, unusual expressions such as 'effulgence', 'express image', 'substance', 'place of repentance', 'builder and maker', and the method of dealing with Scripture, are said to be Alexandrian. Certainly both writers argue from the silence of Scripture and attach importance to the meaning of Old Testament names. Yet there is a tendency to overrate the Alexandrian influence on the Epistle through a desire to locate the author in Alexandria. Moreover, the treatment of the Old Testament by our author is different from Philo's and, therefore, is not necessarily Alexandrian. Philo used the Old Testament simply as a peg for mystic allegory, whereas for the author of Hebrews the persons and institutions of the Old Testament are types, rudimentary and imperfect anticipations of the new covenant but never merely symbols. Even Philo's elaborate exposition of the tabernacle seems different from what is found in Hebrews, and there is little evidence to support the suggestion that our author's thought about Melchisedec was drawn from Philo. For example, he made use both of Genesis xiv and Psalm cx, and this latter passage, so far as is known, was never used by Philo. In Hebrews Christ is portrayed as Mediator of creation,

---

[1] *A New Commentary on Holy Scripture*, Vol. II, p. 596.

revelation and redemption, as well as Mediator of the new covenant. Philo, through his emphasis on God as pure spirit, and through the influence of Plato's dualism, not only divorced God and matter, but maintained that without mediation of some kind God could not act upon matter. This is a departure from the biblical point of view and from our author (cf. ii. 10). Westcott stated that Philo's theory of the word standing between the creature and the Father of all, the messenger of divine order and the inspirer of human life, is the finest relation of the world to its maker apart from the incarnation. Yet for Philo the word, or divine logos, was nothing more than a philosophical abstraction, and very different from the living Word who is the personal Mediator of the new covenant. The writer may have been, and probably was, familiar with the ideas and philosophical terminology to which the Alexandrian school of Jewish philosophy gave wide currency in the first Christian century. There is, however, no evidence in his work to show that he was a disciple of the Alexandrian school, but at the most he may have made free and independent use of words and ideas hailing from that quarter, just as far as they would serve his purpose. Yet most of his thoughts could have been drawn from the Old Testament, the Wisdom literature of the Apocrypha, and Jewish apocalyptic thought, with all of which Paul himself was familiar.

Any one of these arguments, whether based on style and vocabulary, or the theological differences between this Epistle and St. Paul, or on the supposed Alexandrian connection, would not be strong enough by itself for us to reject the Pauline authorship; but the cumulative evidence is most convincing, especially against direct Pauline authorship.

If Paul did not write Hebrews then who was the brilliant first-century writer who produced this outstanding work? Ramsay suggested Philip the Deacon; Harnack, Priscilla and Aquila; Chapman, Aristion; but there is so little evidence to support such views that they may be passed over. A good deal has been said about Clement of Rome being the author, but although there is an early reference to his connection with the Epistle, it seems very doubtful whether a man of Clement's calibre could have written such an outstanding Epistle as Hebrews. This leaves us with four other names worthy of consideration—those of Barnabas, Apollos, Luke and Silas.

Tertullian was the first to ascribe the Epistle to Barnabas. The work (*De pudicitia 20*) in which his assertion is found, was most probably written at the close of the second century or at the beginning of the third. This tradition, therefore, is almost as old as the Alexandrian. Was Tertullian the originator of this ascription or did he rely on some tradition? Zahn suggests that he found the Epistle so described in a MS which came from some Greek source.[1] There is just a possibility that *Barnabae Epist.* in Codex Claromontanus means 'The Epistle to the Hebrews', but it is far more probable that it means 'the Epistle of Barnabas'. The appellation 'son of exhortation' or 'consolation',[2] which the apostles placed upon Barnabas (Acts iv. 36) shows that he may have had the necessary qualifications for writing 'the word of exhortation' (Heb. xiii. 22). The same verse in Acts describes him as a Levite and, therefore, it is only natural to assume that he was well-acquainted with the Levitical ritual which plays such an important part in the Epistle to the Hebrews. Barnabas was also a native of Cyprus, and as this land is closely connected with Alexandria, it is highly probable that he would be acquainted with Alexandrian thought and terminology. There is a tradition which associates Barnabas with Alexandria.[3] There would also appear to be an assumption that he was the author of the Alexandrian Epistle[4] that bears his name, and if this is correct then it is almost certain that Barnabas was not the author of Hebrews.

[1] *Einleitung in das N.T.*, 845.
[2] See F. F. Bruce, *The Acts of the Apostles* (Tyndale Press), p. 130.
[3] Cf. Clem. *Hom.*, i. 8, ii. 4.
[4] *Encyclopaedia Britannica*, Vol. III, 11th edition, p. 408.

Moffatt points out that Barnabas' relation to the original gospel was probably closer than that implied in Hebrews ii. 3. It is true that a tradition exists which suggests that Barnabas was one of the seventy, but this may have arisen from the confusion of the names Barnabas and Barsabas (Acts i. 23). Tertullian in *De pudicitia* 20 says, *qui ab apostolis didicit*, and if Barnabas was a disciple of the apostles then he could easily fit into the circumstances envisaged in ii. 3.

Moffatt further asserts that the rise of the Pauline tradition is inexplicable if Barnabas, or indeed any other name, had been attached to the Epistle from the first. As Moffatt rejects the Pauline authorship, and all other names are excluded, the Epistle can only be anonymous; but there is not the slightest indication that the author wished to conceal his personality, and if the author of Hebrews has become anonymous to later Christians, he was not anonymous to the readers (cf. vi. 9 f., x. 34, xiii. 7, 9).

Nairne thinks Tertullian's suggestion of Barnabas has the appearance of being an inference from the subject-matter of the Epistle. Tertullian's suggestion was never accepted in Cyprus, the native country of Barnabas; nor in Africa, Tertullian's country; nor anywhere else in the Church.

Luther did not like the Epistle to the Hebrews because he believed that it taught that there was no second repentance. He placed it with one or two others at the end of the New Testament, thus making a distinction between them and the rest. It might appear from this that Luther questioned the canonicity of Hebrews, but the fact that he placed it among the New Testament books suggests that he was not prepared to oppose the decision of the Church by completely rejecting it. He did, however, disallow the Pauline authorship and was the first to suggest the name of Apollos as the possible author. Certainly Apollos belonged to the second generation of Christians, for he was taught the deeper truths of the Christian life by some of Paul's friends (see Acts xviii. 26). It would also

appear that he had some intimate contacts with Paul himself.
As a Jew he was well-versed in the Jewish Scriptures, and as
a native of Alexandria he would have accurate knowledge of
the Alexandrian mode of typological interpretation of the
Scriptures. Luther's suggestion has won much favour and
recently has been strongly supported by T. W. Manson (who
suggests that it was written to the communities of the Lycus
valley[1]) and by W. F. Howard.[2] There are, however, one or
two serious objections against it. There is no evidence that
Apollos was ever in Rome or had any contact with the Church
of Rome. Moreover, as W. Manson rightly points out, 'if
Apollos had been the author, it is difficult to think that the
Alexandrian Church would not have preserved some knowledge of the fact in view of the distinguished role of this son of
Alexandria in world-mission; and that Clement would not
have mentioned him in writing to the Corinthians in whose
history Apollos had played a notable part.' Furthermore, the
Alexandrian Christians from the earliest times assigned the
Epistle to another person.

Luke seems to have been considered as the writer by Clement
of Alexandria on the grounds that the purer Greek of Hebrews
resembled his, and because the Epistle contains words and
phrases found elsewhere in the New Testament only in St.
Luke's Gospel and the Acts. Luke, moreover, was a companion
of Paul, and there is the tradition known to Origen that Luke
was the actual writer. Moffatt offers some serious objections to
Lucan authorship. After a careful examination of the language
he finds only six words peculiar to Acts and Hebrews, and only
two (*diabainō* and *diatithemai*) which occur in all three docu-
ments. There is in addition a conspicuous absence from
Hebrews of several characteristically Lucan words and phrases.[3]
Another serious objection to the Lucan authorship is the

[1] *The Problem of the Epistle to the Hebrews*, John Rylands Library Bulletin
xxxii. 1–17, Manchester, 1949.
[2] *The Epistle to the Hebrews: An Interpretation*, January 1951.
[3] *Introduction to the Literature of the New Testament*, p. 436.

well-founded assumption, based on a comparison of Colossians iv. 14 with Colossians iv. 11, that Luke was a Gentile Christian, whereas most scholars admit that the author of Hebrews was a Jew. These facts would seem conclusive against the original authorship of Luke, but they need not exclude him from having had some part in the composition of the Epistle. It is evident that he did not translate a Hebrew original, for Hebrews, as we have it, can hardly be a translation.

It has been suggested that the whole style and structure of Hebrews are more like a spoken discourse than an Epistle. It is pointed out that it is not unlike Paul's synagogue addresses, and that it is just possible that the Epistle is one of Paul's discourses, and that Luke has recorded it in his own way. Luke would not be so familiar with the Aramaic as with Greek, and would therefore prefer the LXX. This theory, it is claimed, may account for Clement's statement, and also for the view of certain modern scholars that Luke had a part in the composition of the Epistle. We are not certain however that Luke was not familiar with the Aramaic, for in chapters i and ii of his Gospel many Aramaisms occur. And although these may be due to a faithful reproduction of the sources used by Luke rather than the product of his own hand yet, as F. F. Bruce remarks, 'If Luke was indeed a native of Antioch, he might well be acquainted with Aramaic, which was spoken in the hinterland of that city . . .'[1]

Silas has been suggested because of the striking coincidences between 1 Peter and Hebrews. Silas, according to some scholars, may have been the amanuensis of the one and the author of the other. Clogg seems to dismiss this on the grounds that Silas is not associated with Hebrews by tradition. This, however, seems to beg the question: for, if modern scholarship is to confine itself to traditional names, then only Paul, Barnabas, Luke and, possibly, Clement need be considered, and the evidence is more strongly in favour of Paul than the

[1] *The Acts of the Apostles* (Tyndale Press), p. 7.

others. Modern scholarship, however, has rejected the Pauline authorship.

We must therefore pass in review such information as we possess about the personality and activities of Silas, to see whether there are any grounds to support the claim that he was the author.

Silas is most probably the Jewish and *Silvanus* the Latin form of his name. We learn from Acts xvi. 37 that, like Paul, he was a Roman citizen. In the description given in Acts xv of the Council at Jerusalem Silas' name appears for the first time, and he is described as belonging to the 'chief men among the brethren' (Acts xv. 22). He was commissioned along with Judas Barsabas by the apostles and elders to write the Council's decisions and to take the letter to Antioch and explain its contents. Shortly afterwards he is attached to Paul and becomes an ardent supporter of the world-mission. He accompanied the apostle on his second missionary journey, and both were imprisoned at Philippi. He was with Paul at Corinth where 1 and 2 Thessalonians were most probably written. It is maintained by some scholars that Silas was the actual writer of these Epistles on the grounds that the letters are addressed to the Thessalonians in the joint names of Paul and *Silvanus and Timothy* (1 Thes. i. 1; 2 Thes. i. 1), and that the first person plural of authorship is found with the occasional incursion of the first person singular. Apart from an isolated reference in 2 Corinthians i. 19, there is no further reference to Silas in the history of Paul. In fact there is only one other mention of him in the New Testament outside of Acts, and that is in 1 Peter v. 12, where he seems to be associated with the writing of 1 Peter. There are therefore four passages which suggest that he had a part in the production of some document, i.e. if the Silas of Acts and the Silvanus of 1 Peter are one and the same person.[1]

[1] Lightfoot in his *Notes on the Epistles of St. Paul* carefully points out that the Silvanus who was the bearer of St. Peter's first Epistle is most probably the Silvanus of St. Paul's letters, but that the name is too common to allow of the identity being pressed.

Selwyn looks upon Silvanus not only as the bearer of 1 Peter but also as the draughtsman. He maintains that if he were the bearer only, *epempsa*, 'sent', not *egrapsa*, 'have written', would have been the more natural word.[1] But Selwyn goes further; and maintains that there are striking affinities between the Epistle to the Hebrews and 1 Peter. Some of the words and phrases, he thinks, may be more than fortuitous. Thus *geuesthai*, 'taste', in vi. 4, 5 may, in view of its context, be derived, as in 1 Peter ii. 3, from Psalm xxxiv; and *eulogian* with *klēronomein* in Hebrews xii. 17 and 1 Peter iii. 9 may have a similar connection. The injunction to 'pursue peace', *eirēnēn diōkete*, in Hebrews xii. 14 has also, as in 1 Peter iii. 11, the same source. The idea of the Church as the *oikos*, 'household', of God presided over by Christ as High Priest (Heb. iii, x. 21) is similar to the neo-Levitical conception underlying 1 Peter ii. The classical word *komizesthai* occurs in Hebrews x. 36, xi. 39 and in 1 Peter i. 9, v. 4 in contexts so similar as to strike the attention, and to suggest that it may have been almost a *vox technica* in the early Church.

There are other words and phrases which appear to reflect similarities of doctrinal development or of historical circumstances behind the two Epistles. 'The Word of God is living' (cf. Heb. iv. 12) recalls 1 Peter i. 23. Jesus is the 'Shepherd' in Hebrews xiii. 20, as in 1 Peter ii. 25. In Hebrews i. 2, as in 1 Peter i. 20, the revelation of God in Christ has occurred 'at the end of' the times or days, and is regarded as an eschatological event. There is a particularly close affinity in the doctrine of the atonement, as we find it in Hebrews ix and 1 Peter ii, iii, and in the terms used in connection with it. Christ was *amōmos*, 'without spot' (Heb. ix. 14 and 1 Pet. i. 19); He suffered for sins *hapax*, 'once' (Heb. ix. 28; 1 Pet. iii. 18); He bore (*anēnegken*) our sins (Heb. ix. 28; 1 Pet. ii. 24); His blood was 'blood of sprinkling' (Heb. xii. 24; 1 Pet. i. 2). Even the characteristic Petrine idea of the *imitatio Christi* has an echo in Hebrews xii. 1, 2. Both Epistles were written in the context of

[1] *The First Epistle of Peter*, 1946, p. 241.

persecution. Hebrews xiii. 13 (cf. also xi. 26) contemplates Christianity involving reproach (*oneidos*) no less than 1 Peter iv. 14, and the lesson is given in both cases (Heb. x. 29–31, 37 f.; 1 Pet. iv. 17–19) that God will take the Church's cause into His own hand and vindicate His own. In such circumstances Christians could scarcely be other than 'strangers and pilgrims on the earth', like the patriarchs of long ago (Heb. xi. 13; 1 Pet. i. 1, ii. 11).

'I cannot get away from the impression', remarks Selwyn, 'of a relationship between Hebrews xiii and 1 Peter, which goes beyond what common sources or common doctrinal tradition, or even common circumstances, will explain. There seem to be the same problems of Church life, and the same attitude to them behind both—the same need of hospitality, or sympathy, of active well-doing, of inner cohesion, and subjection towards the Church's leaders; the same sense of reproach and of being without a settled earthly home; the same necessity to imitate Jesus in His suffering; the same hope of an inheritance awaiting believers at the last. And the great chapter of Hebrews reaches its climax in words redolent of 1 Peter, and of 1 Peter when most near to 1 and 2 Thessalonians.'

Is it not possible, says Selwyn, that among 'those from Italy' (Heb. xiii. 24), who were beside him when he wrote, there was one who had been the close associate of St. Paul in writing to Thessalonica and of St. Peter in his first Epistle? The hypothesis would do much to explain the intimate links which seem to bind Hebrews and 1 Peter together.[1]

The possibility exists, therefore, that Silas may have had a part at least in writing Hebrews, i.e. if he satisfies the other conditions.

1. We know that the writer and readers were known to each other (vi. 9, xiii. 18, 19, 23, 24). Now whether the readers were Hellenistic Jewish Christians at Jerusalem or Rome they would be known to Silas, who had connections with both places. If *Babylon* in 1 Peter v. 13 refers to Rome, as the weight

---

[1] Selwyn, *op. cit.*, pp. 463–466.

of the evidence seems to suggest (cf. Rev. xiv. 8, xvii. 5, etc.), then Silas had contact with Rome.

2. Hebrews xiii. 23 shows conclusively that Timothy was known to writer and readers. According to 1 Thessalonians i. 1, 2 Thessalonians i. 1 and 2 Corinthians i. 19 Silas was known to Timothy, and it seems that Timothy was with St. Paul at Rome and would therefore be known to the Church there.

3. The writer was familiar with the Levitical ritual system. Before Silas joined the world-mission he was attached to the Church at Jerusalem, and being a Jew would be well-acquainted with the ritual of the temple. The suggestion of discrepancies in this connection in vii. 27, ix. 4 (fully dealt with in the Commentary) cannot be taken as conclusive evidence against Silas.

4. The writer of Hebrews was a classicist who constantly made use of the LXX. The writer of 1 Peter exhibits a felicity of phrase, suppleness of expression, and a wealth of vocabulary which betoken a mind nourished in the best Greek spirit and tradition. He is deeply steeped in the Jewish Scriptures, as he shows both by direct quotation and by frequent indirect allusions, and he knows them in the LXX form.[1]

W. Manson asserts that the key to the Epistle is to be found only by examining the history of the world-mission of Christianity from its inception in the work of Stephen. He sees the first breach within Christianity between the gospel on the one hand and the temple and law on the other. He also suggests that the teaching of Stephen is not only the matrix within which the theological ideas elaborated in Hebrews first took shape, but indirectly explains 'the existence of a minority in the Roman Church who in reaction from the larger freedom of the world-mission gospel were asserting principles and counter-claims akin to those of the original "Hebrew" section in the Hebrew Church'.

C. F. D. Moule, though far from accepting every aspect of

[1] Selwyn, *op. cit.*, p. 24.

Manson's view about the world-mission, accepts in Stephen's speech the easily recognizable likeness to the thought of Hebrews.[1]

The book of Acts leaves us in no doubt about Silas' part in the world-mission and, therefore, he would be acquainted with the speech of Stephen. In fact it is highly probable that he heard Stephen deliver his speech,[2] and it is possible that he was Luke's source for an account of it.

The background and personality of Silas, his circumstances, theological thoughts, style and vocabulary are not against the theory that he was the author of Hebrews, and may even support it. He may have arrived in Rome with Peter about AD 63 and witnessed the condition of the Church there. Paul was a prisoner in Rome at the same time, and it is almost certain that Silas would pay a number of visits to his friend. While with Paul he would undoubtedly discuss the difficult circumstances of the group within the Roman Church. He may have taken down notes of Paul's answer to the situation. At the beginning of AD 64, however, he was sent with 1 Peter to the Christians living in Asia Minor. While there he may have heard of the martyrdom of Peter and Paul, and of the crisis arising within the Church. He may, therefore, have written the Epistle to the Hebrews at this time, using Paul's notes as a foundation. He may also have made use of patterns of teaching and collections of the 'words of the Lord' drawn up under the apostle's and prophetic guidance. Furthermore, he would have a perfect knowledge of the tenets of the world-missions as a background. He may have sent a covering letter to the separatist movement within the Roman Church explaining how the Epistle came to be written.

---

[1] *Theology*, Vol. LXI, No. 456, pp. 229–230.
[2] According to Selwyn Silas' name appears in the lists of the 'Seventy' (Luke x) found in Ps.-Dorotheus (6th century), but its inclusion there may be purely guesswork. It may be argued that if Silas was one of the 'Seventy' then his knowledge of the gospel would be more direct than what is implied in ii. 3. Even if this were true, it can be argued that writers often identified themselves with their readers.

The Jewish Christians may have made a complete break from the main stream of the Church in Rome, and could, as Manson suggests, 'have disappeared completely'. On the other hand, some years after AD 75 one or two of them, having seen the fulfilments of the statements in the Epistle (cf. viii. 13), may have rejoined the rest of the Church bringing with them the Epistle to the Hebrews and claiming that it was from Paul. This claim, however, was rejected on the grounds of dissimilarity of style, and of the remote possibility of Paul writing a letter to a separatist movement.

It may be argued that this is merely a hypothesis, and with this one must agree. The data at our disposal does not amount to proof and the authorship of the Epistle, therefore, must remain hypothetical.

II. THE READERS OF THE EPISTLE

The evidence at our disposal strongly supports the view that the readers were Jewish Christians.

1. Even though the title *pros hebraious* (to the Hebrews) may not be original, it must belong to a very early tradition for it is found in the MSS Vaticanus and Sinaiticus and in the Chester Beatty papyrus. Moreover the person who added the title certainly believed that the Epistle was addressed to Jewish Christians. The internal evidence shows that it was not written to Hebrews in general but to a definite society or group of readers, who had steadfastly endured persecution and suffered the loss of property, though they had not 'resisted unto blood' (x. 32–34, xii. 3, 4). Their sympathy towards their imprisoned brethren had issued in good works (x. 32–34, vi. 9 f.). According to v. 11–vi. 3 the readers were still 'babes' whereas they ought to have been 'teachers', and some of the leaders were dead (xiii. 7), showing that the Church had been in existence for a considerable length of time. There is also a strong suggestion that they were not settled in the faith, and as a result they were in danger of drifting.

2. The writer constantly appeals to his readers from their own Scriptures—the Old Testament. Reference is made to the old covenant, to Melchisedec, to types and shadows, and throughout the Epistle it is taken for granted that the readers would be quite familiar with the references. It seems that much of this would have little point if the Epistle had been addressed to Gentile Christians. Röth in 1836, followed by Von Soden, Moffatt, Scott and others, reject this, and claim that it was written to Christians in general, or Gentile Christians. E. F. Scott went so far as to say that among modern scholars the opinion is gaining ground that the explanation of the Jewish colouring is unnecessary. The facts, however, are against this, and only a few modern scholars are inclined to this point of view.[1] His further assertion that to Christians of the first century the Old Testament was the one acknowledged Bible, no less than to the Jews, and formed the natural basis of any attempt to present Christianity as the religion of the new covenant, has found little support. The weakness of the statement has been clearly shown by the fact that the acceptance of the Old Testament by Jewish and Gentile Christians rested on quite different grounds. The Jews accepted it because they were Jews, the Gentiles accepted it because they had embraced Christianity. Now if the latter broke with Christianity then the Old Testament would lose its interest for them, whereas if these Jews should leave Christianity the Old Testament would still have some value for them, and therefore an appeal to it could still be made.[2] Scott is on firmer ground when he suggests that the Epistle was written to an inner circle in a church, probably in Rome. Its instruction is more detailed and its teaching more advanced than would be natural for ordinary Christians. A teacher, so Scott assumes, is here communicating a Christian *gnosis* to a select circle of disciples, to give them a

---

[1] W. Manson has made an excellent and convincing criticism of the various points put forward in support of this modern theory in *The Epistle to the Hebrews*, pp. 18–23.

[2] Editor's note, *Peake's Commentary on the Bible*, p. 889.

truer and deeper conception of Christianity beyond the bare elements with which they were already familiar.

The Epistle hardly suggests, however, that the readers were advanced enough to be able to assimilate the deeper truths of Christianity (cf. v. 11–vi. 3), though it does suggest that the readers constituted a small group within a large society. The members of this group are exhorted not to forsake the common Christian assembly (x. 25) and to obey those who have the rule over them (xiii. 17).

F. D. V. Narborough[1] suggests that the danger which threatened the readers of Hebrews was similar to the false teaching which was opposed by Paul in Colossians. He maintains, therefore, that they were Gentile Christians who lived in the vicinity of Ephesus. But why should the writer lay so much stress on the Levitical and the sacrificial system if the readers were Gentiles being led astray by gnosticism? Stibbs makes the suggestion that they were a group of Jews who had been members of the Dispersion. They were zealously devoted to Judaism, and possibly while on a visit to Jerusalem both writer and readers embraced Christianity.[2] Others maintain that this group may have been part of the Christian 'dispersion' which followed the martyrdom of Stephen (Acts viii. 1, xi. 19).

The Epistle may be anonymous to us but, as is sometimes forgotten, both writer and readers were known to each other. There is no suggestion in the Epistle that the writer wished to be anonymous (xiii. 19). Furthermore, Timothy seems to have been known to both readers and writer (xiii. 23). It is also highly probable that the readers were a small group within a larger society and separated from the leaders, and there is a suggestion in x. 25 that they were beginning to forsake the common Christian assembly. It is, therefore, possible from these statements and from what has been said before to conclude that the readers were Jewish Christians, probably resident in Rome.

[1] Commentary in *The Clarendon Bible*.
[2] *The New Bible Commentary* (Inter-Varsity Fellowship), p. 1089.

III. THE DESTINATION OF THE EPISTLE

The various suggestions concerning its authorship have gone
hand in hand with various suggestions for the destination of
the Epistle. Alexandria has been suggested because it is claimed
that the outlook and thought of the writer are supposed to be
Alexandrian and follow the tradition of Philo. If it could be
proved that Apollos was the author, then this suggestion would
have considerable weight. But are the outlook and thought of
the writer Alexandrian, and does the author follow the
traditions of Philo? It has already been shown that sometimes
on both these points there has been undue exaggeration.

Some of the scholars who support the authorship of Barnabas
have suggested Antioch as the place of destination. But would
the same scholars suggest Antioch if Barnabas were not the
author? In a similar way Caesarea has been suggested on the
grounds of the Lucan authorship.

It has been asserted that the Fourth Gospel, which is supposed to emanate from Ephesus, has the same kind of philosophy as is found in our Epistle; and that it is therefore reasonable to maintain that Hebrews also was sent to the same city.
But this seems to build too much on too little. The thought of
the logos doctrine seems to pervade both books, and Hebrews
may be nearer than the Paulines to the Johannine logos. To
build identity of destination, however, on a doubtful identity
of philosophy is not convincing.

From very early times Jerusalem has been suggested as the
destination of the Epistle. Both Chrysostom and Theodoret
supported this theory, and in recent times it has been upheld
by Heigl, de Wette, Delitzsch, Tholuck, Bloomfield, Ritschl
and others. The reasons given in support of Jerusalem as the
place of destination are firstly that the title *Pros Hebraious*
more naturally denotes Jewish Christians in Palestine than
anywhere else, although the word *hebraious* can be used in an
ethnic as well as a linguistic sense. If it is used here linguistic-
ally then it must refer to Palestine, for Aramaic was not spoken

outside Palestine. In contradistinction to such Hebrews, those who came from the Diaspora and spoke Greek were called Hellenists. According to F. F. Bruce the strict Jerusalem Jews boycotted the use of Greek, cultivating the vernacular Aramaic.[1] In the 'ethnic' sense the word refers to all who belonged to the twelve tribes (Acts xxvi. 7). Secondly, Ebrard, who also supports Jerusalem, thought that it was written to encourage Christian neophytes there, who were rendered anxious by being excluded from the temple worship and from participation in the sacrifices.

There are, however, some weighty objections against Jerusalem. The Hebrew Christians to whom the Epistle is addressed had been evangelized by those who heard the Lord, suggesting that the readers had never heard Jesus (ii. 3). Would this be true of those who lived permanently in Jerusalem? Nairne seeks to overcome this difficulty by suggesting that the readers may have been Hellenistic Jews who had settled in Jerusalem. Moffatt admits that the force of this argument may be met by admitting that the circle addressed is not the whole Church, but a Hellenistic section of it, but, he maintains, the censure of v. 12 would be singularly inapplicable to any section of the mother-church of Jerusalem at any period, even after AD 70.[2] Furthermore, the readers here had 'not yet resisted unto blood' (xii. 4), but this could not be said of Christians in Palestine. The impressive past history of the community addressed, which is to be found in vi. 10, x. 32–34, xiii. 7, seems rather to support the Roman destination, though it is doubtful whether such conditions were confined to the church at Rome.

There are two facts which must be borne in mind when discussing this problem. First, the Epistle was written either to, or from, Italy. The more natural meaning of the phrase *hoi apo tēs Italias*, 'they of Italy' (xiii. 24), is 'Christians from Italy who, living outside Italy, send greetings to their friends in Italy'. It

---

[1] *The Acts of the Apostles* (Tyndale Press), p. 151.
[2] *Introduction to the Literature of the New Testament*, p. 446.

may mean, however, 'Christians in Italy', in which case the destination of the Epistle would be outside Italy.

Secondly, the first traces of the Epistle are found in the work of Clement of Rome and in others connected with Rome. As Clement wrote in AD 96, then the Epistle was known in Rome at that time, and this fact suggests, but by no means proves, as Moffatt shows, that Rome was probably the place to which the Epistle was sent.[1] With this conclusion W. Manson concurs: 'There is', he says, 'the notable absence, both in Hebrews and Romans, of all reference to gnostic and heathen errors on the part of Christians counselled. The only erroneous teaching which is commented upon in Hebrews concerns food-laws, and this is a point in curious agreement with St. Paul's Romans, where the same, or similar, doctrines are attributed to a section of the Roman community.'

IV. THE DATE OF THE EPISTLE

It has already been mentioned that this Epistle was known and used by Clement of Rome in his letter to the Corinthian Church. It is generally agreed that Clement wrote about AD 96; therefore the Epistle to the Hebrews was written some years before Clement wrote his letter. There is no other external evidence which is of value in the fixing of a date, but the internal evidence is much more helpful.

If we knew for certain that the purpose of the writer was to urge Jewish Christians to remain loyal to Christianity and to break completely from Judaism during the strain of the circumstances of the Jewish war, then the date could be placed definitely before AD 70 when Titus sacked Jerusalem. In support of this, there is the allusion in the present tense to the Old Testament ritual system as if it were still in operation. But the use of verbs in the present tense is not conclusive in itself, for such usage continued after the destruction of Jerusalem in a few writers. It has also been asserted that the author is not dis-

[1] *Introduction to the Literature of the New Testament*, pp. 446, 447 footnote.

cussing the sacrificial system of the temple but of the tabernacle, which perished hundreds of years before the time of
writing this Epistle.

Even if this argument could be maintained, the fact remains
that the tone of warning to the readers against being drawn
back to Judaism seems to pervade the whole Epistle, although
Scott and Moffatt would not assent to this. If the Jewish war
had taken place and the old system had vanished, is it conceivable that no mention would have been made of such
catastrophic events by the author, especially when the whole
situation would have given conclusive proof to his arguments?
This would support the view of a date before AD 70, when the
Jewish temple was destroyed. There are certain factors which
suggest that the Epistle cannot be very early. The readers appear to be of the second generation of Christians, for the gospel
was confirmed unto them 'by them that heard' the Lord (ii. 3).
It would also appear that those who first brought the gospel
to them had died (xiii. 7). The Church had been in existence
for some time, and there had been growth in numbers and
development, but certain members who should have been
teachers were still in spiritual infancy (v. 12).

The author speaks of their past achievements in ministering
to the saints, which they did for Christ's sake (vi. 10). Further,
in two important passages (x. 32 and xii. 4) he speaks of days
of persecution which they could look back upon, though they
had not yet resisted unto blood. W. Manson suggests that the
situation envisaged in x. 32–34 took place in AD 49, the year
of the Claudian edict imposing extradition on the Jews of
Rome, and maintains that the language of xii. 4 implies that
death for the faith will have to be reckoned with as a real con-
tingency of the Christian calling. A date about AD 60 would
be sufficiently removed from the events of AD 49 to allow the
author's reference to them as 'the former days', but would also
be prior to the Neronian persecution when actual martyrdom
was experienced by the Church. These verses are interpreted
by Manson on the assumption that the Epistle was written to

Christians in Rome. Manson's identification of the 'forty years' period of the divine probation of Israel after the Exodus with a similar period of Christianity from the time the word was 'spoken by the Lord' would suit a time nearer AD 65 than AD 60.

Moffatt and Scott, who deny that the readers were Jewish, assert that the Epistle was written to a group of Gentile Christians, and date it about AD 80 to 85. It seems, however, that the situation in which the readers found themselves was one of crisis, such as is suggested in Luke xxi. 20, 21. It is also possible that the author sees in this crisis the inevitable end of the old Levitical system (viii. 13). A date nearer AD 65 would seem best to meet the various lines of evidence.

V. OCCASION AND PURPOSE

The writer's purpose was to a large extent influenced by the circumstances and spiritual condition of those to whom the Epistle was addressed. Chapter xiii. 7 gives the impression that the readers had been attached to Christianity for some considerable time, long enough for them to have become full grown men in the faith. They ought by now to have been teachers, but they were still babes and in need of teaching themselves (v. 11, 12). Their daily spiritual diet should have been the strong meat of Christian doctrine. But not only were they in no condition to receive this; they were fit to receive baby-food only. This low mental and spiritual grasp of the Christian faith was blinding their minds to the true nature and value of Christianity. Furthermore, they had become grieved at, and absorbed with, their sufferings. But, in assessing the writer's aim, there are also other factors which must be considered.

The Jewish nation had become hostile to Christians and no longer was it possible for the latter to worship within the temple precincts. This exclusion of the Christians from the law and temple seems to have affected the readers and was partly responsible for their discouragement. It is also possible that the Jewish nation was facing a serious crisis and was making a strong appeal to all Jews for their help and loyalty. Over against this there was the appeal of the Christian Church which finds expression in the gentle suggestion of the writer that they should break with Judaism (xiii. 13).

They were thus face to face with a serious dilemma which had arisen because they had neither fully broken from Judaism nor fully embraced Christianity. According to Wickham, 'these Jewish Christians' had become 'what we call in St. Paul's Epistles Judaisers'. Even if this statement is not altogether correct, the evidence strongly supports the view that the author is giving a full and systematic answer to the Judaistic controversy. Our Lord had clearly taught the universalism of the gospel by pointing out that the new wine of His teaching could find no lasting place in the old skins of Judaism (Mk. ii. 22). Stephen seems to have been the first among the early disciples to discern that a break between official Judaism and Christianity was inevitable (cf. Acts vi, vii). Paul also saw clearly that there could not be a Jewish Church and a Gentile Church, but one Christian Church. He also grasped, as Stephen did before him, that a break from the law and temple was inevitable. The author of Hebrews has gathered all these together and, with exceptional skill and tact, has given a full, rational and systematic answer to this difficult problem which faced the infant Church in general and his readers in particular. The Epistle to the Hebrews, however, can never be limited to any age, for it must ever remain the classic answer to the dangers of sacerdotalism.

The author's main method of dealing with such a situation is to stress the finality of Christianity, and its superiority over all other religions. He seeks to accomplish this by a comparison of those two religions which claimed divine revelation— Judaism and Christianity. This is not to say that he had no interest in other religions; but from his point of view no religion could be compared with those two whose origin was the direct result of God's initiative. 'The author's idea of Christianity', according to H. B. Bruce, 'is that it is the best possible religion; but what he sets himself to prove is that it is better than the Levitical religion. It is not difficult, however, to read between the lines, and to see behind the apologetic better the dogmatic best.'[1]

The author commences his treatise by a comparison of the two religions and by examining them as two revelations from God. While there is no disparagement of the old revelation, for it was God-given, its imperfection is clearly seen in its fragmentary and shadowy nature because of the limitations of those agents through whom the revelation came. On the other hand, the superiority and perfection of the Christian revelation lies in the agent Himself, who is God's Son, perfect in Himself, perfect in His knowledge of God, perfect in His function as revealer of God.

The sudden transition from the comparison of the two revelations and the agents through whom the revelations came to a comparison of Christ and angels may suggest that an effort is being made to counteract the development of Jewish angelology. It is more probable that he is moving towards the subject of mediation. His consciousness of God's holiness and his knowledge of man's sinfulness have convinced him that, if man is to draw near to God, mediation of some kind is absolutely essential. The centre of the law for the writer was to a large extent the system of ritual and sacrifice through which the people drew near to God. The giving of the law, however, was held by the Jews to be the greatest inspiration of the old revelation and it came through a twofold mediation. Moses, who received the law and passed it on to the people, had it delivered to him by an angel or angels (cf. Acts vii. 53; Gal. iii. 19; Heb. ii. 2). It is possible that these angelic bodies were looked upon as the highest of God's creatures. It was necessary, therefore, to show that the revelation through them was inferior to the revelation in Christ. This the writer does

[1] *Dictionary of the Bible*, II, p. 327.

41

by bringing out the surpassing dignity of the Son while at the same time showing that the angels were merely servants. He further points to the kingship of Christ and to the angels as subservient. He is the Creator while they are His creatures sent forth to serve the heirs of salvation.

For Moses the writer had nothing but respect, for was he not known as the great lawgiver and the deliverer of Israel from the bondage of Egypt? Yet even Moses was only a member of the house, but Christ was the builder. In the same house Moses was called the faithful servant, but Christ was recognized as the faithful Son. After a brief exhortation in which the 'rest' to be found in Christ is seen to be better than the 'rest' provided by Joshua (iii. 7–iv. 13) the writer shows that the priesthood of the Son is superior to the Aaronic priesthood. This is the only book of the New Testament which refers to the priesthood of Christ. The fact that the writer refers to Christ as 'priest', 'high priest', 'great high priest', does not necessarily mean that there is some subtle meaning in the use of such terms. By the use of the two latter expressions it is almost certain that he is seeking to bring out Christ's surpassing eminence in His priestly character. Four qualifications were necessary for a valid priesthood. The one who filled the office must possess a nature common to mankind, for he was to be taken from among men. It was necessary for him to be chosen by God in order to manage the religious interests of his fellowmen. A further need was a compassionate nature that he might deal gently with those who erred. He must also have something to offer that would bring lasting benefit to the sinner. These qualifications Christ certainly possessed (v. 1–10).

For the writer a priest is a person through whom, and through whose ministry, people draw near to God. The main object of the priesthood was, therefore, to bring men into abiding fellowship with God. The Levitical ritual fails to do this for two reasons. First, the characters of the mediators were imperfect. They were men of many infirmities and, in consequence, had to offer for their own sins before they could offer for the sins of the people (v. 3). Second, the sacrifices which they offered were imperfect, for it is not possible that the blood of bulls and of goats should take away sins (x. 4).

It was sin which had created the barrier between God and man, and until this barrier was removed there could be no permanent access into God's presence. The repetition of the sacrifices year by year was proof that this problem of sin had not been solved once and for all. Further evidence is seen in the fact that even the high priest could enter into God's presence only on one day a year. He had no abiding access. The people had no access whatever, the veil stood between them and God.

The superiority of Christ over the Levitical ritual system and its mediators is now brought out in numerous ways. The writer first of all makes use of the priesthood of Melchisedec which existed long before the institution of the Levitical priesthood. It is almost certain that he was seeking to overcome the difficulty of the accusation that as Christ did not belong to the tribe of Levi He could not be a priest. The writer does so by pointing out that there was another priesthood of the most high God recognized in Jewish history—a royal priesthood (Gn. xiv; Ps. cx). This priesthood is superior to the Levitical, for it is ancient and even Abraham, who represents the unborn Levi, paid honour to it.

The superiority of the character of Christ's priesthood, which is after the order of Melchisedec, is further emphasized by the statement that it is based on an unchangeable and eternal divine oath (vii. 20). No such oath was ever connected with the Levitical priesthood. Then the rule of Christ's priesthood rests in the power of an indissoluble life (vii. 16), and the very fact that He abides for ever shows that His priesthood does not pass to another (vii. 24). No such statements could be made of the Levitical priests for they were continually removed by death. His character is superior, for though He was in all points tempted like as we are, yet He was without sin (iv. 15). The importance of this sinlessness should be realized for, as Denney rightly says, 'The sinlessness of Jesus entered into the atonement: Only one who knew no sin could take any responsibility in regard to it which would create a new situation for sinners . . .' It would be impossible to transfer the consequences of sin from the sinner to Christ if He had been in the same condition as other sinners and the Levitical priests.

The character of His offering was also superior and this is clearly brought out in ix. 13, 14 and x. 10–12. Christ made only one offering, whereas in the Levitical ritual the offerings were many. His offering was an intelligent act of the highest spiritual obedience to God and not the sacrifice of an irrational dumb animal. He offered Himself through the virtue of His eternal spiritual nature which made the offering of infinite value and accomplished eternal redemption. It did not, therefore, cancel the errors of a twelvemonth, but removed for ever the barrier of sin between God and man. On this perfect sacrifice, which was offered once and for all by the perfect High Priest, the perfect and absolute covenant was established.

The term covenant, which occurs seventeen times in this Epistle, is twice said to be better than the old covenant, three times it is said to be a new covenant—new in time and new in quality—and once it is declared eternal. The inauguration of the new covenant was proof that the first covenant was not faultless in its moral code nor in its ceremonial and political institutions. The value of the moral law lay in its revelation of the sovereign authority of God in the giving of the law, of His holiness in the nature of the law and of the complete ruin of sinners under it. Its limitations and ineffectiveness are seen in the continued failure of the Israelites to keep the covenant, and the ineffectiveness of the law to enable them to keep it. It demanded perfect obedience from the people and condemned them for any transgression (ii. 2).

The limitations of the ceremonial institutions have already been given. All that need be said here is that this aspect of the covenant kept alive the hope that God would raise up a seed of Abraham who would bring deliverance to the people and save them from ruin. The many priests pointed to the great

High Priest, the many sacrifices to the one perfect Sacrifice, the limited access to God to the ever open way whereby man may have continual fellowship with God.

The purpose of the political institutions is to be found in the promise of the Messiah who was to be of the seed of Abraham. It was necessary, therefore, to distinguish the people of Abraham, and set them apart from the other nations, by peculiar institutions and ordinances of worship. They were to be God's people and God was to be their King. Hosea and Jeremiah saw the end of this relationship under the old covenant through the constant failure of the Israelites. It was the inauguration of the new covenant which brought to an end the national existence of Israel as God's chosen people. In a sense the Jewish nation's cry, 'we have no king but Caesar', was the end from the human side. Israel is now under a new covenant which includes all nations and peoples.

The new covenant provides Christians with a law of inward spiritual power which enables them to keep the covenant (viii. 10). Its predominant blessing is the forgiveness of sins (viii. 12), which enables the sinner to have free and permanent access to God's presence (x. 19, 22). The one all-sufficient guarantee of this new covenant is based upon the greatness of Christ's person, the all-sufficiency of His sacrifice, the superiority of His priesthood, the authority behind His resurrection and His ascension to the throne of God.

ANALYSIS

I. THE INTRODUCTION (i. 1–4).

II. THE SON SUPERIOR TO ANGELS (i. 5–ii. 18).

    a. The Son's superiority supported by the Old Testament (i. 5–14).

    b. An exhortation and a warning (ii. 1–4).

    c. The Son's superiority not cancelled by His humiliation (ii. 5–13).

    d. The Son's superiority not marred by suffering (ii. 14–18).

III. THE SON SUPERIOR TO MOSES (iii. 1–iv. 13).

    a. The Son and Builder superior to the servant and member (iii. 1–6).

    b. The second warning (iii. 7–19).

    c. The gospel of rest (iv. 1–13).

IV. THE MERCIFUL AND GREAT HIGH PRIEST (iv. 14– v. 10).

    a. Our gracious and sympathetic High Priest (iv. 14–16).

    b. The qualifications of a true priest (v. 1–4).

    c. The validity of Christ's priesthood (v. 5–10).

V. SPIRITUAL PROGRESS (v. 11–vi. 20).

    a. Spiritual infancy (v. 11–14).

    b. The need to 'go on' (vi. 1–3).

    c. The third warning (vi. 4–8).

    d. Comfort and hope founded upon God's promise (vi. 9–20).

COMMENTARY

I. THE INTRODUCTION (i. 1-4)

THE majestic and impressive opening forms an introduction to the Epistle as a whole. The main purpose of the writer is to show the absolute supremacy of the gospel revelation in the Son, who has accomplished a full and final reconciliation of God and man, over the imperfect revelation in the prophets. Both these revelations came from the same source. Both had the same divine origin—God; and the same divine purpose, fellowship between God and man, lay behind both. God unveils Himself that man may know Him and draw near to Him. The person, office and glory of the Son are brought forward as proof of His superiority.

1. God is the subject of the sentence but it is unnecessary to place His name first as the AV has done. It has no support from the Greek, and it tends to obscure the contrast between the two revelations. 'In many and various ways God spoke' (RSV) is better, but *polumerōs, at sundry times*, and *polutropōs, in divers manners*, do not enlarge one and the same idea, but show that it was in many degrees and in different ways that *God . . . spake in time past*. These two words, *polutropōs* and *polumerōs*, according to Davidson, signalize the variety and fulness of the Old Testament word of God. Yet the prophetic revelations were fragmentary, occasional and progressive, for no single one of them, nor all of them, contained the whole truth. The fact that man is responsible if he sins constitutes, perhaps, the original revelation (cf. Gn. ii. 16, 17). Further revelation was given to the patriarchs, to Moses and to the prophets. God spake by dreams and visions, by typical ordinances, by angels and especially by the law and prophecy.

All such revelation was *in time past*, or 'of old', for Malachi, the last of this prophetic order, had died more than four hundred years before Christ came. It was given *unto the fathers*, i.e. to the Jewish people, for to them were committed the oracles of God. Yet these oracles did not come directly to them, for God spake *by the prophets* (literally 'in the prophets'). *Prophētai* must not be confined to the later prophetic order, or to Moses and the prophets; it must be taken in its widest sense to cover all those holy men of Old Testament history who received revelations from God. The use of the preposition *en*, 'in', and not *dia*, 'through', shows that the prophets were not mere instruments. God was dwelling in them, controlling and quickening them that He might make known His divine will and purpose. Nairne points out that when our author says 'God spake in the prophets' he is not likely to have intended less than the fullest inspiration of most *reasonable* heralds.

2, 3. The final revelation of God *unto us by his Son* was, and is, an eschatological event, for it came *in these last days*. As *eschatou*, *last*, is singular, 'at the end of these days' (RV) is better. When Christ came the old era was fulfilled and the new age dawned; the final and eternal order became operative in the incarnate Son and the new-born Church; and it will continue to be so until the consummation of all things. *Unto us*, therefore, need not be confined to the author and his readers, but includes all believers.

The supreme dignity of the person in whom God spake is expressed by the phrase *by his Son* (literally 'in a Son') or, as Westcott rightly suggests, 'One who is Son', for it is the *nature* of the agent of the Christian revelation which is under discussion. The old revelation is thus inferior to the new, for the prophets who were mortal and sinful men had neither the authority nor the dignity of the Son. Nor had the message of the law and the prophets either the effective power or the excellency of the gospel message.

The Son's greatness is now illustrated through His relation to the universe, to God and to humanity.

The phrase *whom he hath appointed heir of all things* not only expresses the ultimate purpose of God in creation but also reveals the Son as the Sovereign Lord of the universe. The AV has correctly used the English perfect tense here to translate the Greek aorist, for no definite time is in mind. As the Sonship is eternal, so the appointment to the inheritance belongs to the eternal decree of God.

Christ is also the instrumental cause of creation, for God through Him *made the worlds*. The Jews spoke of three worlds: (i) the upper world (the habitation of God), (ii) the middle world (the air), and (iii) the lower world (the earth). It has been suggested that the writer had this in mind when he spoke of *worlds*. The Greek, however, literally means 'ages' and signifies that Christ is the creative Mediator of the universe in all its successive phases, whether past, present or future. Delitzsch understands 'ages' as the immeasurable content of immeasurable time.

Christ is the perpetual support and guiding principle of all creation, for He upholds *all things by the word of his power* (verse 3). There is nothing static in this, for the Son of God by His omnipotent word is bearing the universe as it moves onward to the consummation. The early Christians strongly believed in the doctrine of divine providence and purpose. The view that God created the world yet did not make its continued existence assured was unknown among them. They taught that in Christ all creation was sustained; that in Him all creatures live, move and have their being; that in Him the universe is moving forward to its destined end; and that in Christ the believer has a share in the glory which is to be revealed in God's own time.

Christ has already been called God's own Son. He is now described as *the brightness* (or 'effulgence') *of* God's *glory*. *Apaugasma, brightness*, is found in Wisdom vii. 26, and occurs frequently in Philo, but only here in the New Testament. It is understood in two ways, as 'radiance' or 'reflection'. Here the meaning is 'radiance'. Just as the rays of the sun reveal the glory of that celestial body and are identified with it, so Christ radiates the glory of God and is identified with Him. The Son is further described as *the express image of his person*, the very counterpart of the Father, or 'very God of (i.e. 'out from') very God'. He alone could say 'he that hath seen me hath seen the Father' (Jn. xiv. 9). As Westcott says, 'He brings the divine before us at once, perfectly and definitely according to the measure of our powers.' Not all see the Son as 'the light of light', 'very God of very God', for the Godhead veiled in flesh is only perceived by the eye of faith.

God has revealed Himself in His Son and the Son reveals God to mankind. God speaks in His Son and the Son speaks to humanity. He is thus God's prophet, but He is also God's Word, the message as well as the Messenger, for the very substance of the gospel is Christ. He is God's Priest acting on behalf of man, for *he . . . by himself purged our sins*, or 'by Himself made purification'. Christ by this one sacrifice of Himself has brought about a permanent purification of sins, which the Levitical priests were unable to do. Here is to be found the essential truth that He who fully reveals God fully redeems man. The words *by himself* are understood by some scholars to be a gloss; the RV also omits them. Wickham says, 'They have little manuscript authority and are omitted in the R.V. Although when the doctrine of Christ's sacrifice had been developed they would be appropriate, they would at present be premature.' Notwithstanding the weight of this objection, it is difficult to accept it, for the following reasons: (i) Throughout the Epistle we find similar phrases, such as 'by his own blood' (ix. 12), 'by the sacrifice of himself' (ix. 26), 'when he offered up himself' (vii. 27). (ii) The evidence of the manuscripts in favour of this phrase is stronger than one is often led to believe. (iii) This reading may have been used in early days to support the spurious reading 'without God' (ii. 9), which may account for its omission in some MSS. Zuntz maintains that the original reading is *di'hautou*, 'through Himself'; and that it combines two meanings, or rather two shades of one meaning, (a) 'by His own virtue and effort, with no assistance from outside'; (b) 'not through an agent but through, or in, His own person'.

The completeness of the great work of purification is seen in the next movement of Christ, which was from the cross to the crown, from earth's footstool to heaven's throne where He sat down at the right hand of God. This well-known language taken from Psalm cx. 1 proclaims His dominion over the whole world and shows His supreme dignity. The Son came to earth in humiliation, but by such condescension revealed His Father to humanity. He died on the cross, but in so doing opened the gateway of life to sinners. He ascended to heaven, and there reigns not only as King of the Jews, nor as man's King, but as Sovereign of the universe.

4. It has been indicated that the God-given revelation in the Son surpasses that given in the prophets. According to Jewish belief Moses occupied the highest place amongst these Old Testament mediators, and Jewish history associates angels with Moses in the giving of the law (Dt. xxxiii. 2; Acts vii. 53; Gal. iii. 19). Moffatt is right when he suggests that the sudden transition to a comparison between the Son and the angels implies that something specific is occupying the writer's mind. Yet the suggestion that an effort is being made to check the tendency of incipient gnosticism with its deference to angels is doubtful, for that would appear to have arisen later than the date of this Epistle. He may have been dealing with the development of Jewish angelology, of which proofs are not lacking in contemporary Jewish literature. But, as his main purpose was to show the superiority of the Christian revelation over the Jewish, and as the angels played a considerable part in the latter, it was necessary that a comparison with the Son should be made so that their inferiority could be seen by the readers. By the use of *genomenos*, 'is made', and not *ōn*, 'being', it is made clear that Christ's superiority in His *eternal* existence is not in mind. It was in virtue of His work of redemption in time that Christ was exalted and occupied the throne, and thus became more excellent than the angels in power and dignity. Previous to His exaltation He was made through His incarnation a little lower than the angels. Nowhere in Scripture is it recorded that an angel was to be the Messiah, but prophecy witnesses to the fact that the incarnate Christ would be the Son, a name signifying pre-eminence over the angels (verse 5). Westcott challenges the objection that the title 'Son' is not limited to the Messiah in the Old Testament. He says, 'The title which is characteristic of Messiah is never used of angels or men in the Old Scriptures. Angels as a body are sometimes called "Sons of God" (Ps. xxix. 1, lxxxix. 6) but to no one is the title "Son of God" given individually in all the long line of revelation.'

II. THE SON SUPERIOR TO ANGELS
(i. 5–ii. 18)

By a variety of arguments the author indicates how the Son is more excellent than the angels (5). He supports these arguments by seven quotations from the Old Testament (6–14). A warning is interjected (ii. 1–4). The author then shows that Christ's temporary humiliation, which was for man's redemption and glorification, did not detract from His pre-eminence over angels (ii. 5–18).

a. The Son's superiority supported by the Old Testament (i. 5–14)

5. The author, taking it for granted that the readers had acknowledged and accepted Jesus as the Jewish Messiah, introduces a quotation from the unmistakably messianic Psalm ii by the statement that it was God the Father who said, *Thou art my Son*. These words may have a primary reference to some Israelite king, possibly Solomon, but there are certain aspects

of the Psalm which cannot be limited to any earthly monarch.

If *this day* refers to God's eternal day, then *have I begotten thee* must refer to Christ's eternal Sonship. The expression is sometimes connected with the baptism of our Lord (Lk. iii. 22, Western text), or with the resurrection (Acts xiii. 33; Rom. i. 4), or even with the transfiguration (Mk. ix. 7). It is highly probable that this association of baptism, transfiguration and resurrection with Psalm ii. 7 created the Ebionite idea of the progressive exaltation of Christ, who, from the Ebionite viewpoint, was just an ordinary man; the three great events in His life were simply stages in His gradual deification. But our Lord is 'Son of God' not by creation, nor by adoption, nor by any office, but by nature, for He is the eternal Son of God who 'In the beginning . . . was with God, and . . . was God . . . and . . . was made flesh, and dwelt among us' (Jn. i. 1, 14). As verse 2 states that the world was created by the Son, the Son must of necessity have existed before the foundation of the world.

There is no Hebrew equivalent for *Let all the angels of God worship him* in our existing text. It may be derived from Psalm xcvii. 7 'worship him, all ye gods' (Heb. *elohim*). The LXX has 'angels' instead of 'gods'. The quotation, however, is exactly found in Deuteronomy xxxii. 43 (LXX), though this may be an addition by a later hand.

The second quotation *I will be to him a Father, and he shall be to me a Son* is derived from 2 Samuel vii. 14. David had in mind the building of a temple for the Lord, but God's prophet, Nathan, points out that laudable though such a scheme might be, it was God's purpose that it should be built by his seed whose kingdom and throne He would establish for ever. Though this quotation primarily referred to Solomon, it has a further reference to the advent of a theocratic King.

6. The words *And again, when he bringeth in the firstbegotten into the world*, introducing another quotation, have been interpreted by some as referring to the incarnation, when, according to Luke ii. 13 f., the angels worshipped Jesus. Others have applied them to His resurrection and exaltation. It has also been suggested that they imply that, just before the incarnation, God the Father took His Son to the created beings and presented Him as the First-born and Creator-ruler. The order of the Greek words is against these suggestions, for there is a close connection between *and again* and *when he bringeth*. The translation is therefore 'And when he again bringeth the first-born into the world'. The reference would seem to be to the second advent of Jesus Christ and to the establishment of His messianic kingdom. *Prōtotokos*, *firstbegotten*, derives its meaning to a large extent from the context in which it is found, but 'priority' and 'superiority' are nearly always associated with it. In Romans viii. 29 Christ is 'the firstborn among many brethren'; in Colossians i. 15 'the firstborn of every creature'; and in Colossians i. 18 'the firstborn from the dead'. It would appear that only in the passage before us is it used without limitation and is descriptive of honour and dignity. At the time when God leads His firstborn a second time into the world and His glory is revealed, the angels are called forth to worship Him who was made for a season a little lower than themselves.

7, 8. Some commentators have taken *O God* to be nominative, either subject or predicate. If subject, the translation would be 'God is thy throne for ever and ever'. If predicate, 'Thy throne is God', or 'the foundation of thy throne is God'. Such translations sound very strange and have no parallel elsewhere. The AV, RV and RSV rightly support the vocative and translate *Thy throne, O God*. Yet Bengel goes too far when he says, 'They clearly do violence to the text who hold the opinion that it is the nominative case in this passage', for the LXX admits of both interpretations. Addis suggests that the original was 'thy throne, O Yahweh', but that this was changed to 'thy throne, O God'. He then claims that Yahweh was itself a mistake of the scribe for 'will be', and concludes that the text should read 'Thy throne will exist for ever and ever'.[1] There is little or no MS evidence to support this, and it seems an ingenious guess to avoid the identification of Christ with God.

In both verses 7 and 8 God is stated to be the speaker and verse 7 must be taken in direct contrast with verse 8. The author uses two quotations, one from Psalm civ. 4 and the other from Psalm xlv. 6, 7. The translation of the Hebrew of the former passage would be 'God makes winds His messengers, and flames of fire His servants'. The LXX, which is followed by the author, has 'He makes His angels winds, and His servants a flame of fire.' The use of the Greek word *poiōn, maketh,* implies the creaturely nature of angels and the possibility of their mortality, whereas the Son is begotten, not made, and abides for ever. Some have suggested that God often clothes the angels 'with the changing garment of phenomena', transforming them, as it were, into winds and flames. It is better to take the *angels* as God's messengers clothed with God's powers to accomplish His will in the realm of nature. To achieve this end they are allowed to co-operate with the storm winds and flames of fire as they did on Mt. Sinai. But however important and exalted their service, and however perfect its performance, they are still the messengers and subjects of God. *The Son,* on the contrary, is addressed by the Father not as a messenger but as God, who occupies an eternal throne, and as Sovereign, who rules His kingdom with righteousness. As *euthutēs, righteousness,* bears the opposite meaning to crooked, 'uprightness' or 'rectitude' would be a more correct translation. A crooked sceptre was an emblem that the administration was unjust; therefore Christ's sceptre, which is upright, shows that His administration is always right and just.

9. *Thou hast loved righteousness, and hated iniquity* is not an expansion of the latter part of the previous verse, but a reference to the life and ministry of Christ while on earth (cf. Phil. ii. 7–9). *Therefore,* i.e. because the God-man loved righteous-

[1] Peake, *Commentary on the Bible,* p. 380.

57

ness and hated iniquity, *God, even thy God, hath anointed thee.* It is possible, as in the previous verse, to translate 'O God, thy God hath anointed thee'. The anointing does not refer to the pouring of the Holy Spirit upon Christ, but to the outpouring of blessedness and glory which took place after His voluntary humiliation and suffering. This anointing most probably followed the resurrection and ascension, and its object was to invest Christ with universal sovereignty and dominion, for He had proved Himself by life and character to be worthy of such rule. In the original Psalm *above thy fellows* refers to the contemporary kings and rulers of other lands. In this passage it includes all those who have fellowship with God; but as the main purpose of the writer in this section is to emphasize Christ's superiority over the angels, *above thy fellows* would seem to refer especially to them.

10–12. The quotation in these verses is taken from Psalm cii. 25–27, a Psalm which gives prominence to the intervention of God on behalf of His people to save them from earthly calamity. While the old covenant was still standing the Jewish people were under God's protection—they were His people. But the breaking of the covenant meant the end of His protection. In the New Testament God again intervenes, for 'God was in Christ, reconciling the world unto himself' and delivering His people from their sins (2 Cor. v. 19; Mt. i. 21). In the Psalm the address is plainly to God, and there is no reference whatever to the Son, the word 'Lord' not being in the original, although it is found in the LXX which may account for its use here. For this reason some scholars have denied any reference to the Son, and maintain that it refers to God the Father, and that the argument put forward by the apostle is merely that 'The perpetuity of the Messiah's throne is secured by the eternity and immutability of God'. While it is true that there is nothing in the Psalm to mark its application to Christ, the writer was nevertheless using a method of Old Testament exegesis which would be readily understood by the people of his day. As Westcott says, 'The application to the Incarnate Son of words addressed to Jehovah rests on the essential conception of the relation of Jehovah to His people. The Covenant leads up to the Incarnation.'

First, the Son is set forth as the Creator of the universe, for He *laid the foundation of the earth*, a figurative term for creation. Secondly, He is sovereign over the changes of the universe for *as a vesture* He shall *fold them*, or roll them, *up*. (On this final consummation cf. Mt. xxiv. 35; 2 Pet. iii. 7; Rev. xxi. 1.) Thirdly, He is the unchangeable Lord amid the changing universe, for *they shall perish* but Christ remains. Though the world grows old like a garment and moves on to dissolution, this does not necessarily mean the annihilation of the universe. The verse simply states that its present form and use will be changed and that the Son will make the changes. Other changes had taken place and were taking place which greatly affected the Jews. The old covenant between God and Israel had come to an end, the Levitical ritual was about to vanish away and the Mosaic law was to undergo a change. Yet the Son in time and in eternity never changes, nor do His years ever come to an end. He is always 'Jesus Christ the same yesterday, and today, and for ever' (Heb. xiii. 8).

13. A final and crowning quotation from Psalm cx is now brought forward as proof of the Son's complete sovereignty. The messianic character of this Psalm is supported by Jewish testimony, by apostolic witness, but above all by the authority of Christ Himself (Mt. xxii. 41–44). It is the Father who gives the invitation to the Son to *Sit on my right hand*. Such an invitation was never extended to angels, for such honour and dignity was never theirs either by right or by gift; it belonged to the Son alone, who possessed it by right in His pre-existent state and now takes it by invitation; it had been reserved for the One who had completely finished His work on earth and was about to begin His ministry of intercession in heaven.

The Father's work in co-operation with the Holy Spirit

would continue in heaven and earth until all the Son's enemies were placed under His feet. The illustration is taken from the ancient custom of conquerors putting their heels on the necks of their vanquished foes in token of their complete subjection. There is no suggestion in the use of the word *until* that when all Christ's enemies were vanquished He would cease to reign. It is equally legitimate to translate the Greek word 'while' as well as *until* (cf. Mk. xiv. 32, where our Lord commands His disciples: 'Sit ye here, while I shall pray').

14. Service, not dominion, is the function of all angels, to whatever class they may belong, for *are they not all ministering spirits? Leitourgoi, ministering,* may express service to God, while *eis diakonian, to minister,* may refer to service to men; but this deduction is doubtful here for *diakonia* implies service to God for the sake of those who are *heirs of salvation,* or who are about to inherit salvation, i.e. for those who enter into a state of salvation on earth and receive its full fruition in heaven.

The author's use of the word *salvation* follows the pattern of other New Testament writers. In xi. 7 where it is recorded that the ark was a means of delivering Noah and his family from the flood, the meaning differs little from the earlier books of the Old Testament (cf. Jdg. xv. 18; Ex. xiv. 13; Acts vii. 25). The same idea of physical deliverance occurs in the deliverance of the Israelites from the Babylonian experience (Is. xlv. 17), but in this we see the beginning of the messianic deliverances. In our Epistle the main use of the word, however, is spiritual and it acquires a twofold meaning: (i) deliverance from evil and the result of evil—death; (ii) power to do what is right, with the bestowal of certain blessings. The former is found in such passages as ii. 3, ii. 10, v. 9 and vi. 9 where Christ is pictured as the Captain and Author of eternal salvation enabling His people to attain their true destiny to have dominion over both the forces of evil and creation. The believer is thus saved once and for all from the consequence of sin through the death of Christ; and, because this salvation is eternal, he cannot therefore experience eternal death. The full realization of the blessedness of salvation awaits the believer in the world to come (ix. 28), but as he is an heir of salvation (i. 14) he already partakes of this blessedness. Thus he is saved from the power and fear of death, from the practice of sin, and from the customs, spirit and love of the world, being succoured when tempted (ii. 18), having a conscience purged from guilt (ix. 14, x. 22), becoming a partaker of the Holy Ghost (vi. 4), entering into God's rest (iv. 1, 3), and inheriting the promises (vi. 12).

b. An exhortation and a warning (ii. 1-4)

1. Although this paragraph is clearly parenthetical, the opening word *Therefore* shows that it is related to chapter i. It is this link which gives greater force to the exhortation and warning. Because of the greatness of His person and the dignity of His office, and the greatness of the revelation which He brought, and His superiority over angels, there rests upon the readers the logical necessity and moral obligation *to give the more earnest heed to the things* which were spoken by the Lord. *The things* is equivalent to the gospel which was brought by Jesus Christ; and *prosechein*, 'to give heed', probably having the opposite meaning to *apistein*, 'to disbelieve', suggests that very close attention should be given to it until its power and authority have convinced the hearers of its truthfulness. Failure to do this carries with it the danger expressed in the words *lest . . . we should let them slip* from our minds (RSV, 'lest we drift away from it'). Both Plato and Sophocles use this verb for things slipping from the memory and becoming forgotten, but probably rightly, the RV and RSV take it in the sense of a drifting boat. The Jews to whom the author is writing were in great danger of drifting away from the truth of the gospel under the pressure of trial and through apathy and indifference (cf. iii. 6, v. 11, vi. 11, 12).

2. A contrast is now made between the word spoken by (or through) angels (i.e. the Mosaic law), which was a revelation of God's justice, and the word 'spoken by the Lord' (i.e. the new law, the gospel), which was a revelation of God's mercy. The object of this contrast is to make plain that the greater privileges of the new revelation carry with them greater responsibilities. God was the author of the Mosaic law, which was held to have been revealed to Moses through angels, although Exodus xix does not in fact mention them. That they played a part at the law-giving was, however, a traditional belief among the Jews (cf. i. 4). (This is confirmed by Acts vii. 53 and Galatians iii. 19.) The old law *was stedfast*, or 'was made steadfast' by the penalties imposed upon those who were guilty of breaking it. Its authority was from God, who required not only that it should be believed, but also that it should be acted upon. Its God-given authority was established by the penalties incurred on the part of those who were guilty of its violation. 'Its commands', says Wickham, 'were enforced, its promises and threatenings came true'. These penalties were applied to every violation of the law, both *transgression*, i.e. doing what the law forbids, and *disobedience*, i.e. neglecting to do what the law commands.

3. By the use of *we*, which is emphatic, the author places himself in the same category as the readers, and expresses in a most explicit way the impossibility of escape by the question *How shall we escape, if we neglect so great salvation?* God was the author of the new law, i.e. the gospel which here is represented as affording, not condemnation, but *so great salvation*, and it was revealed not through Moses or angels but through One who was Son. The superior dignity of the new Mediator is shown by the use of the title *Lord*, and the surpassing exaltedness of the new message over the old is suggested by the words *so great*. Its whole character is spiritual, its blessings and promises are eternal. The privilege of hearing this great message of salvation conveyed by God's own Son far exceeds the privileges of hearing the law given through God's servants. If then the transgressors of the law did not escape the penalty for every breach of that law but received their just reward, how can those under the new law escape God's judgment? The author does not say 'if we reject' but simply *if we neglect*; yet the latter quickly leads to the former. The Greek word (*amelēsantes*) is also used in Matthew xxii. 5 where the invited guests made light of the king's invitation to the marriage of his son, and in Wisdom iii. 10 where the righteous man is lightly regarded. A similar meaning is seen here, for he who neglects God's saving grace in Christ makes light of it as if it were not worthy of his notice. There is no escape for those who so act. God's retribution is sure and 'it is a fearful thing to fall into the hands of the living God' (x. 31). 'Not only the rejection of the gospel', says Calvin, 'but also its neglect deserves the heaviest punishment, and that on account of the greatness of the grace which it offers.' In addition, this gospel was confirmed to the readers by eyewitnesses and ministers of the Word itself. *Ebebaiōthē, was confirmed,* corresponds to *egeneto bebaios,* 'was made steadfast' in verse 2.

The Lord is now stated to be the first herald of the good news, and this is confirmed by the Gospels (cf. Mk. i. 14). Yet the main object of Christ was not to preach the gospel but so to act that there should be a gospel to preach. The dignity of the title *the Lord* brings into vivid contrast the Mosaic revelation which came through angels, and the gospel, or the Christian revelation, which came through the Lord. It has been argued from the phrase *was confirmed unto us by them that heard him* that Paul was not the author of the Epistle. It is true that Paul in Galatians i. 11, 12 claimed to have received his revelation direct from Jesus Christ—'I certify you, brethren, that the gospel which was preached of me is not after man. For I neither received it of man, neither was I taught it, but by the revelation of Jesus Christ.' Yet it is equally true that writers frequently identified themselves with their readers, or with those who were to pass through, or had passed through, some particular experience. Paul says, 'Behold, I shew you a mystery; We shall not all sleep, but we shall all be changed' (1 Cor. xv. 51; contrast 1 Cor. vi. 14). Little can be gained from this verse to help us in deciding the authorship of the Epistle, although both Luther and Calvin argued against the Pauline authorship from this verse; and many modern scholars assume from it that the author belonged to the second generation of Christians.

4. *God also bearing them witness* should be translated 'God bearing witness with them', which is nearer to the original. The divine origin of the gospel which the apostles had confirmed to them, had been made plain by the *signs and wonders, and with divers miracles, and gifts of the Holy Ghost.* This fourfold description is not easy to define because of the close relationship of the phenomena to one another, especially the first three. (i) *Signs* bears witness to the truth of what was preached, so that men's minds may turn to higher things. (ii) *Wonders* describes those events which are rare and unusual enough to arouse interest. (iii) *Miracles* draws attention to the divine or superhuman agency involved. These three words are found together in Acts ii. 22 (though in a different order) and the first two occur in 2 Thessalonians ii. 9. Signs and wonders occur frequently in both the Old and New Testaments, and no doubt refer to those miraculous operations which were common to the law and the gospel. (iv) *Gifts* or 'distributions' of the Holy Spirit refer to such miraculous gifts as are found in 1 Corinthians xii. These were not the same as the signs, wonders and miracles, for they include the word of wisdom and knowledge, the gifts of prophecy, and the discerning of spirits. *According to his own will* does not refer to the Holy Spirit, but to the witness borne by God to Himself.

c. The Son's superiority not cancelled by His humiliation (ii. 5–13)

The argument which was broken off at the end of chapter i is now taken up again, but whereas there the author was discussing the Jews' claim that they had received the law through the instrumentality of angels, he now deals with the objection that Jesus was merely a man who had suffered and died like other men and, therefore, was inferior to the angels. This gives the author the opportunity to investigate further the relation of Christ to the angels and to show that the glorious destiny of man, which was higher than the angels, had its fulfilment in Christ. He also explains the reason why Jesus suffered, died and rose again.

5. *For* connects this section with i. 14. God has ordained that angels should serve the heirs of salvation and not rule *the world to come*. There is also an important link through the word 'salvation' with ii. 3 and 10. The Son of God, by whom so great salvation was proclaimed and through whom they became 'heirs', is also the Captain of their salvation appointed to lead the heirs to their true destination and inheritance.

Some have understood *the world to come, hē oikoumenē hē mellousa*, as having the same meaning as in the verse 'Nevertheless we, according to his promise, look for new heavens and a new earth, wherein dwelleth righteousness' (2 Pet. iii. 13). Others, in associating it with the celestial state, have given it a similar meaning. In vi. 5 the expression *the world to come* occurs again, but instead of *oikoumenē* (the inhabited earth), *aiōn* (age) is used. The expression most probably carries the same breadth of meaning as 'at the end of these days' (i. 2, RV). Such terms as these have extensive meanings, embracing the entire divine activity to bring about the salvation of man. Calvin remarks, 'the world to come is not that which we hope for after the resurrection, but that which began at the beginning of Christ's Kingdom, but it no doubt will have its full accomplishment in our final redemption.' Whatever meaning is applied to the phrase it is not put in subjection to angels. This does not imply that the old order was in subjection to angels; it merely states that the new order will not be in subjection to them but to Christ, the Son of man.

6. The divine purpose for the new order that it should be ruled by man and not by angels, is foretold in the Old Testament for *one in a certain place testified* of this very purpose. This indefinite mode of expression, which was constantly used by Jewish writers, does not imply that the place of Scripture in question was unknown to the author. Both he and his readers were well acquainted with Psalm viii which describes the high destiny for which man was created. It is difficult to decide from the words *What is man, that thou art mindful of him?* whether the author has in mind the dignity of man because God is mindful of him, or the insignificance of man amid the magnificence of creation. Certainly this latter meaning has the support of Psalm cxliv. 3 which shows man's emptiness and worthlessness, though he is the subject of God's care. *The son of man* should not be distinguished from 'man', for this form of expression is merely due to Hebrew parallelism.

7. Three things are now mentioned in connection with God's purpose for man. First *thou madest him a little lower than the angels*. The use of the aorist tense favours 'thou didst make' (RSV). It also expresses a definite divine act in the ages that are past which made man a little lower than the angels. In the Hebrew and Greek the word *little* has both a local and a temporal significance. It is the latter which is used in our text and 'for a little while' (RSV) is to be preferred. In Psalm viii, in place of 'a little lower than the angels' (LXX), the Hebrew text has 'a little less than God (*Elōhim*)'. If the Hebrew text be followed, then it could mean that man was made a little less than God, or a little below the glory of God, or as Westcott puts it, 'a little less than one who has a divine nature'. Some modern commentators deny the messianic character of Psalm viii, asserting that the quotation simply refers to the material dominion of man. It is true that there is reference to such a dominion, yet in the light of man's sin and failure the author relates it to the spiritual and universal dominion of the representative Man, Christ Jesus, through whom this passage receives its fulfilment. Secondly, as 'man' in Psalm viii was crowned king of nature, for God set him over the works of His hands, *crownedst* must refer to the King's coronation with glory and honour. Yet when related to Christ in the present context it has a twofold meaning, referring to the King's coronation which took place when He ascended to the right hand of the Majesty on high, and also to the Victor's coronation which was bestowed upon Him as the great Conqueror of sin and death (cf. Eph. iv. 8). The words *thou . . . didst set him over the works of thy hands* are omitted by some of the best MSS, and as they are not relevant to the author's purpose they should not be included. There was a tendency amongst later copyists to reintroduce into the text the familiar LXX wording where alterations or omissions of this text are found in the New Testament writings.

8. Thirdly, the original decree that God has *put* (or 'did put') *all things in subjection* to man has never been rescinded; it still stands. Nothing is to be left outside man's sovereignty except God. In the original passage the psalmist amplifies *all things* by stating 'all sheep and oxen, yea, and the beasts of the field', and Genesis i. 26, 28 states that he is to have dominion over the fish of the sea. But *all things* in this passage refers to the universal dominion of Christ. Man, though for a short time made lower than the angels, was—and is—destined to occupy the highest place amongst God's creatures, and even angels are to come under his dominion; but this will only be realized in and through the Man Christ Jesus. It is highly probable, as some suggest, that the Psalmist did not understand the full significance of what he was recording, but this has little point. According to 1 Peter i. 10–12 many things were hid from the prophets which have now been revealed to us.

The words *But now we see not yet all things put under him* are not found in Psalm viii. They are a simple deduction from obvious facts whether they refer to man or Christ. The divine purpose has not been fulfilled in man; the sceptre has slipped from his grasp; he has failed to realize his sovereignty. Moffatt remarks that the terror of death and the devil enslaves human nature. But it is more consistent to refer the words to Christ, for though He occupies the throne, His kingdom is not fully established and many enemies still exist. Yet the eye of faith perceives Jesus already crowned with glory and honour. It is this experience which brings supreme hope to the Christian—that the divine promise that man should be triumphant, a promise which has never been withdrawn, will be accomplished.

9. The accomplishment of man's triumph began with a period of humiliation, for Christ *was made a little lower than the angels. Little* here is little in degree rather than 'little' in time. There was also a time of suffering and death, and an act of coronation which crowned Him with glory and honour so that His death might be efficacious for the redemption of every sin.

Some commentators have suggested that the coronation and incarnation were a necessary prelude to His passion. In this case Christ was crowned for death, but when did this act of coronation take place? Randall suggests that it took place in His pre-existent state in the councils of eternity. Bruce associated it with the transfiguration which was closely connected with His death, and suggested that it could be described as a crowning in preparation for His suffering, giving merit to His death. Others have associated the crowning with God's approval at Christ's baptism and transfiguration. It is better to adopt the rendering of the RSV which states that Jesus was crowned with glory and honour because of the suffering of death, thus making His exaltation a necessary sequel or reward of His death. This is similar in meaning to Philippians ii. 8, 9: 'he humbled himself, and became obedient unto death, even the death of the cross. Wherefore God also hath highly exalted him . . .' The exaltation was necessary for the perfection of His redemptive work for, as Alford rightly says, 'On the triumphant issue of His sufferings their efficacy depends.'

Should taste death means not only that He died (cf. Mt. xvi. 28 and Jn. viii. 52), but that He tasted all the humiliation and bitterness of death. He experienced the wages of sin *for every man*. Origen (and others) accept *pantos*, *every man*, as neuter and maintain that Christ tasted death for every existence, i.e. the universe. Support for this aspect of the atonement can be found in Ephesians i. 10, but it is out of harmony with the personal emphasis of this whole section which lays particular stress on the individual aspect of the atonement (cf. ii. 16). Moreover, the use of the singular, *pantos*, in preference to the plural, *pantōn*, favours the masculine reading that Christ died not for mankind in general, or as a totality, but *for* (or 'on behalf of') each single individual. The meaning of *huper* with the genitive is 'on behalf of', but this does not necessarily mean that substitution should always be excluded from the word. Paul seems to use *huper* in 1 Timothy ii. 6 with the same meaning as *anti*, 'instead of'. As he is quoting from Mark x. 45, it is inconceivable that he would deliberately alter the meaning of the word used by our Lord. A. T. Robinson goes further and says, 'The author (of Hebrews) interprets and applies the language of the Psalm to Jesus and here puts Christ's death on behalf of (*huper*) and so, instead of, every man as the motive for His incarnation and death on the cross.'

It is strange that there is no reference to the love of God in this Epistle; the nearest approach is found in the words *by the grace of God*,[1] and in the appointment of a high priest to act for man in his relation to God. The writer's aim was to show the superiority of Christianity; therefore he confines himself to matters relevant to that purpose.

10. The work of Christ on the cross, though a stumbling-block to the Jews and foolishness to the Gentiles, was an act worthy of God. It was in harmony with His eternal nature as moral Governor of the world; it vindicated the rights of divine government violated by man's sin; and it was re-

[1] But see Additional Note on this verse on p. 72.

lated to His divine purpose in bringing the many sons to glory who were destined in Christ to be at the head of all creation.

The expressions *for whom are all things*, and *by whom* (or 'through whom') *are all things* reveal that all creatures come into being through God's creative agency; they exist for His glory; and they find their goal in Him in whom is found all creative and spiritual life. The same preposition *dia*, 'through', is used in i. 2 where Christ's creative agency is discussed. This refutes the charge made by some that Christ was inferior to the Father, because He was simply the agent through whom God created all things. This interchange of attributes between God the Father and Christ the Son suggests, although it does not necessarily prove, the divinity of our Lord.

For *captain* RV has 'author', which is the word used in xii. 2 by the AV to translate the same Greek word *archēgos*. Both these meanings can be found in the use of the word in this verse. Christ is the source, or author, of our salvation; and the association of the word with bringing many sons to glory also suggests that He is *the captain of* our *salvation* leading God's children to the heavenly promised land.

Man was in a state of degradation. He had been appointed to be the head of creation, but had completely failed to fulfil his destiny. Yet God's two-fold purpose remained. In the first place He intended to place man at the head of creation, and in the second, as a corollary of the first, He was determined to bring *many sons unto glory*. This, however, could only be accomplished through suffering, and so Christ suffered. The *captain of* our *salvation* tasted death for every man, and in so doing was made *perfect through sufferings*. This does not mean that suffering cured the Lord Jesus Christ of moral faults. This was impossible, for He was without sin (see iv. 15; cf. 2 Cor. v. 21). The Greek word *teleiōsai* means 'to make adequate' or 'completely effective'. Apart from these sufferings Christ would not have been completely effective in His role of representing and succouring mortal man.

11. The Sanctifier in this verse is the Captain of our salvation, and the sanctified the many sons who are being brought to glory. The sanctified are those who have been made free from guilt through cleansing from sin and who have access into God's presence (x. 10, 14, xiii. 12). *Hagiazein*, 'to sanctify', has almost the same meaning as *dikaioun*, 'to justify', so frequently used by Paul. Denney draws attention to this similarity and then goes on to say: 'The sanctification of the one writer is the justification of the other; and the *prosagōgē*, or access to God, which Paul emphasizes as the primary blessing of justification (Rom. v. 2; Eph. ii. 18, iii. 12), appears everywhere in Hebrews as the primary religious act of "drawing near" to God through the great High Priest (iv. 16, vii. 19-25, x. 22). It seems fair, then, to argue that the immediate effect of Christ's death upon men is religious rather than ethical. In technical language, it alters their relation to God, or is conceived as doing so, rather than their character.'[1]

The sense of *are all of one* is conditioned by 'the sanctifier and those who are sanctified' and, therefore, must not be extended to include all humanity as Paul does in Acts xvii. 26, 28. *Of one* does not refer to their common origin from either Adam or Abraham but to their spiritual origin from God. All Christians are His spiritual children. *For which cause*, though He was of higher rank and different from them, Christ *is not ashamed to call them brethren*. In the scheme of redemption Christ is the firstborn of many sons.

12, 13. Three proofs are here brought forward from the Old Testament to show that Christ is not ashamed to call those who are sanctified—brethren. The first *I will declare thy name unto my brethren* is taken, with slight variation, from Psalm xxii. 22, an unmistakably messianic Psalm which is closely connected with the passion of our Lord as recorded in the four Gospels (cf. Mt. xxvii. 46; Mk. xv. 34; Lk. xxiii. 35; Jn. xix. 24). The messianic character of this Psalm is also recognized

[1] *The Death of Christ* (Tyndale Press), p. 126.

here, where it is related to Jesus Christ who will declare God's name *in the midst of the church* or congregation. Originally verses 22 and 23 of the Psalm referred to some great deliverance of the Psalmist from his sufferings, but here it refers to our Lord's resurrection and exaltation, especially the latter. The second quotation in the present series is taken either from 2 Samuel xxii (cf. Ps. xviii. 2) or from Isaiah viii. 17 (LXX); as the author immediately makes use of Isaiah viii. 18, it is probable that he had the passages from Isaiah in mind. The prophet, as the representative of the people, expresses his confidence in God's word; but our author sees a higher reference to Christ who declares His confidence in God, which is proof of His humanity, and in so doing identifies Himself with His brethren. The third quotation, *Behold I and the children which God hath given me* is derived from Isaiah viii. 18. Originally the passage referred to Isaiah and his children Shear-jashub and Maher-shalal-hash-baz. Our author sees in the prophet a type of Christ and in his children a type of the believing remnant whom He came to save.

Additional Note on ii. 9

Zuntz supports Harnack in rejecting the reading *by the grace of God*, adopting instead of *chariti*, 'by the grace', *chōris*, 'without' or 'apart from'. The following points are put forward by Zuntz to support this variant: (i) Neither through a scribe's confusion, nor by intentional change, could *chōris* have arisen from an original *chariti*. (ii) The motive for changing *chōris* to *chariti* is self-evident; the suffering Saviour, it was felt, could not have been 'separated from God'. (iii) *Chōris* is one of the favourite words of the writer (cf. iv. 15). (iv) This reading agrees with the writer's notion of the passion. Against these points must be placed the following: (i) The MS evidence against Zuntz is overwhelming, for *chōris* is found in only one important Greek MS, namely, 1739. The Patristic evidence is divided and does not help. (ii) Moffatt has pointed out from a Latin version, which has 'gratia', that it may represent an original *charis* which has been changed into *chōris* and *chariti*. (iii) It is more probable that a scribe, knowing the quotation 'My God, my God, why hast thou forsaken me?', could not reconcile it with the statement here that Christ by the grace of God tasted death for every man, and so changed it to *chōris theou* (without God) than that Zuntz' viewpoint on these two texts should be correct. (iv) *Chariti* fits in well with *eprepei* which immediately follows. Professor R. V. G. Tasker in an article-review of Zuntz' work[1] says: 'Here I feel unconvinced by his arguments. It will certainly seem strange to many Christian readers to learn that the statement that Jesus "through the grace of God should taste death for every man yields a preposterous sense". Nor does Zuntz's interpretation of *chōris theou* as "separated from God" appear probable, for surely the writer would have expressed this thought more naturally by *kechōrismenos apo theou*. It would seem more likely, as Tischendorf maintained, that *chōris theou* is a later correction made in the light of 1 Cor. xv. 27, to exclude God from the inclusiveness implied in *huper pantos*.'

The following meanings of the phrase have been put forward by those who accept *chōris theou* as the correct reading: (i) Christ was forsaken by God, in the sense of Mark xv. 34 'My God, my God, why hast thou forsaken me?'. (ii) Christ died apart from His divinity, i.e. when Christ died His divine nature survived. (iii) *Pantos* is taken to mean 'everyone' or 'everything', and therefore Christ died for everyone or everything, but God was excepted. Westcott truly remarks that all these thoughts seem foreign to the context.

d. The Son's superiority not marred by suffering (ii. 14–18)

14, 15. The children are human, for *flesh and blood* ('blood and flesh' is the reading of the best MSS) is a common expression for mankind. They are more than *partakers*, for *koinōnoi* means 'sharers', 'partners'. They are partners in 'blood and flesh', i.e.

---

[1] *New Testament Studies*, Vol. II, pp. 180–191.

partners with Christ who became man, and who voluntarily assumed human nature and united it with the divine nature which He Himself possessed from eternity. The main purpose of our Lord's incarnation was to be the Saviour of mankind, but this could be accomplished only through death, for in this way alone could man's sin and guilt be removed. For reasons not easy to explain, the salvation of God's people through suffering and death was not merely consistent with, but gloriously illustrative of the perfection of divine character, of the principles of divine government, and of the depths and power of divine love.

Here salvation is presented to us in a two-fold aspect—in reference to the great enemy from whom the believer is delivered, and in reference to the bondage from which the Christian is emancipated. *Katargēsē*, *destroy*, means 'bring to nought', i.e. render impotent as though no longer existing. It would appear from this that the devil has had the power of death allowed him because of sin, of which he is the author. Christ by the offering of Himself (see ix. 15, 28) has made a perfect atonement for sin and so brought to nought the power of Satan. The apostle does not say here that Christ has already abolished death itself, but only that He has rendered impotent him that had the power of death. Natural death still remains but it has lost its sting for believers; as Paul says in 1 Corinthians xv. 55, 'O death, where is thy sting?'. He goes on to say that 'the sting of death is sin', implying that the removal of sin ensures that death's sting has been drawn.

16. The object of this great work of Christ was not to save angels but man, therefore Christ *took not on him the nature of angels*. The words *the nature* are not in the Greek and obscure the meaning of the passage. The reading of the AV mg., 'he taketh not hold of angels, but of the seed of Abraham he taketh hold', gives the exact meaning of the Greek. The use of *epilambanetai* ('he takes hold of' or 'he takes by the hand') shows that it is not merely the laying hold of human nature which is in the author's mind, but the rescue and redemption of God's children. A similar use of the verb is found in Jeremiah xxxi. 9 (quoted in viii. 9) where God takes the Israelites by the hand to rescue and lead them out of Egypt.

In the New Testament *the seed of Abraham* signifies the descendants of Abraham, whether natural or spiritual. The phrase is used in the latter sense here, for even though the virtue of the atonement is infinite, its efficacy reaches only those who accept it by faith, and who are described by Paul as Abraham's true offspring (Gal. iii. 7, 9, 29).

17. *Wherefore* may look backward; if so, its force would be, 'Since He is the Saviour not of angels but of men, it behoved Him to be made like unto the brethren'. If it looks forward, its force would be 'For this reason it behoved Him to be made like unto His brethren, that He might be a merciful and faithful High Priest in things pertaining to God to make reconciliation for the sin of His people'.

The words *in all things* should be taken with *made like*, for Christ as man must share in the circumstances, trials, temptations, sorrow and pain of other men. There are notable exceptions, however, to His being made like unto His brethren *in all things*. First, His birth was different, for He was born of a virgin; secondly, His life was different, for He was without sin though tempted with the same temptations that men have to face (see iv. 15); and thirdly, His death was different, for He 'died for our sins according to the scriptures' (1 Cor. xv. 3).

Opheilō, the word here rendered *behoved* was originally connected with financial debts, and meant to owe something to someone, as in Matthew xviii. 28, where one servant owed another an hundred pence. It also had the further meaning of moral obligation, 'ought', or necessity, 'must', which is the meaning of the word here, for there lay upon Jesus a moral obligation to become a man among men, to redeem mankind and to be properly equipped for priestly sacrifice and service.

The word *high priest* occurs here for the first time in the

Epistle. It is also the first time that it is directly applied to Jesus Christ in Scripture, though the expressions, 'made purification for our sins' (i. 3); 'that he by the grace of God should taste death for every man' (ii. 9), and 'both he that sanctifieth and they who are sanctified' (ii. 11) have already prepared the way for its use here. As High Priest Christ was to make reconciliation for the sins of the people, but in the same office He was to be *merciful*, or 'compassionate', to man and *faithful* to God. For *to make reconciliation* the RV has 'to make propitiation', and the RSV 'to make expiation' (cf. ix. 15). The primary duty of the High Priest of sinful men is *to make reconciliation* by the removal of the sin which has created estrangement.

18. The power of sympathy lies not in the mere capacity for feeling but in the lessons of experience for, having suffered *being tempted*, our High Priest *is able to succour them that are tempted*. Furthermore, the power of sympathy does not depend on the experience of sin, but on the experience of the strength of the temptation to sin which only the sinless can know in its full intensity.

III. THE SON SUPERIOR TO MOSES
(iii. 1–iv. 13)

a. The Son and Builder superior to the servant and member (iii. 1–6)

1. The opening word links what has gone before with what follows. Because of Christ's superiority over prophets and angels and because of the greatness of His Person and the effectiveness of His redemptive work, *wherefore, holy brethren, . . . consider* Christ Jesus in the two-fold office of apostleship and priesthood. Under the old covenant these two functions were first held by Moses and Aaron. The ritual aspect associated with Aaron is left over for discussion until chapter v so that concentration may be centred on God's two ambassadors.

The author fully realizes that he is on delicate ground because of the high esteem in which God's old ambassador was held by the Jews. He therefore takes over well-known terms and phrases and with artistic skill and ability spiritualizes them. From Old Testament usage *holy brethren* would be familiar to all Jews. All descendants of Abraham were brethren and Exodus xix. 6 refers to them as 'an holy nation'. But the phrase is now used to suggest that both writer and readers are partakers of a spiritual experience in Christ which has made them sons of God. And while *holy* still retains its original meaning of separation, yet it now has a more ethical significance, for holiness can be accomplished only through separation from sin. The Israelites' claim to be God's chosen people was built upon the fact that they had received a divine call through Moses. The divine call now comes through One who is far superior to Moses. Unlike the former, which was a call to an earthly and temporal inheritance, it is a call to a spiritual and eternal kingdom.

Even the titles *Apostle* and *High Priest* would present no difficulty, for Moses was recognized as God's ambassador to the people and Aaron as man's representative before God. Both these titles are vested in the Son who is the Moses and Aaron of the new covenant.

These Hebrew Christians are urged to consider Christ Jesus who, according to the writer, is the *Apostle and High Priest of our profession* (i.e. of the faith which we confess). They were to concentrate upon this fact until they grasped its full spiritual significance or, as J. H. Moulton suggests, until they 'mastered the mystery'. The full meaning of this confession had obviously been missed by some of the readers, but this is not surprising, for it carried with it results which were of a revolutionary nature for the Jewish mind.

The confession of Christ as God's ambassador carried with it an acceptance of the message, or gospel, which He brought from God and which superseded the law. In a similar way in the confession as High Priest of One who did not

belong to the tribe of Levi lay the rejection of the Levitical
priesthood.

2. Before he sets out to prove the Son's superiority to Moses,
faithfulness, a necessary characteristic of a true ambassador, is
discussed. It was well known from Numbers xii. 7 that God,
who had appointed Moses over all His house (i.e. over the
children of Israel), accounted him faithful in the fulfilment of
that office. The exaltation of Jesus to the throne of God and
His coronation with glory and honour (ii. 9) show that God
has also recognized His faithfulness in the twofold office of
apostleship and priesthood to which He had been *appointed*.
The usual meaning of *appointed* (*poiēsanti*) is 'created'. On this
ground it has been urged that this must be the meaning of the
word in this passage, therefore Christ could not be 'Very God
of Very God'. Even if 'created' be the meaning, it does not
necessarily follow that the pre-incarnate Christ was merely a
creature, for it could refer to His incarnation. Nairne asserts
that 'created' absolutely would—apart from the question of
orthodoxy—bring a superfluous thought into the question. The
context requires the meaning *appointed*, orthodoxy demands it
and 1 Samuel xii. 6 supports it (cf. also Mk. iii. 14 and Acts
ii. 36).

3. The superiority of Christ over Moses is now illustrated by
a discussion on their respective relationships to, and their
positions in, the house. In both these respects *this man* (i.e.
Christ) is *worthy of more glory than Moses*. The relationship of
Christ to *the house* is that of Builder. There is no suggestion here
that Moses is 'the house', nor is there any need to suggest two
separate houses, such as the Jewish and Christian Churches.
'House' in this passage is equivalent to the whole people of God
whether under the old or new covenant. Christ is the Builder
whereas Moses, even though occupying a position of great
importance, was only a member or part of the house. It is
obvious that a part of the house has not the same honour as the

whole, nor has the house the same honour as the builder. Therefore, as Christ is Builder of the house and Moses only part of it, He is counted worthy by God of more glory than Moses.

4. In verse 2 the house is referred to as God's, in verse 6 as Christ's. In verse 3 the Builder of the house is Christ, yet in this verse the Builder of all things is God. This is consistent with the style of the author, who makes no clear-cut distinction between Christ and God. In i. 2 God is referred to as Creator and the Son as creative Mediator of the universe. Yet the same preposition *dia*, which is used with the genitive to bring out the instrumentality of Christ in the work of creation, is used with the same case in ii. 10 to bring out the Father's instrumentality. Furthermore, in i. 10 the Son is spoken of as the Creator who laid the foundation of the earth.

5. The position of Moses in the house is that of a faithful servant. The use of *therapōn* (servant) instead of the more common *oiketēs* (domestic) and *doulos* (bondservant) brings out the intimate relation between God and Moses, and the confidential aspect of his position *in all his house*, i.e. God's house. Although high honour was bestowed upon the great lawgiver, and although he was faithful in the performance of his duties, nevertheless, he was a *servant*, and as such did not abide in the house for ever. His work was indeed transitory, for the fact that he bore testimony to those things which were to come through a greater Apostle revealed its provisional character. Moffatt quite rightly says 'the position of Moses was one which pointed beyond itself to a future and higher revelation'.

6. The final proof of Christ's superiority is now given. He is *son over his own house* and, therefore, is worthy of more glory than the servant. Even though Christ and Moses were both faithful, the position of a son is worthy of more glory than that of a servant, for it carries with it far greater responsibility. The introduction of the word *Christ*, used as an official title and not as a proper name, implies that the Son, the Builder of the house, is the true Messiah. The acknowledgment of Christ as God's Ambassador and all that it implies brings blessings infinitely greater than those which could be obtained through Moses. Yet these can be fully possessed, says our author, only *if we hold fast* our assured Christian confidence and that joyful spiritual hope which should be the guide of the Christian's life.

Firm unto the end is most probably an interpolation from verse 14. In the first place the feminine adjective does not agree with the neuter noun *rejoicing* and is, according to Zuntz, 'syntactically impossible'. In addition, the phrase is omitted in the Codex Vaticanus, the Chester Beatty papyrus and other ancient authorities.

b. The second warning (iii. 7–19)

Moses was faithful but not all those who left Egypt with him followed his example or believed his testimony. Their unbelief was the forerunner of their destruction. Christ, who is far superior to Moses, was also faithful, but many of His followers were not following His example and because of apathy and unbelief were in danger of losing true spiritual blessings. To these a solemn warning is given to show that unbelief leads to disobedience, and unbelief and disobedience to apostasy, and that the inevitable result is the loss of God's rest.

7–9. After *wherefore* some commentators take the rest of verse 7 as a parenthesis, thus reading 'Wherefore . . . harden not your hearts . . .' It is better to follow the AV which, placing in parenthesis the rest of verse 7 and the whole of 8–11 reads 'Wherefore . . . take heed, brethren, lest . . .'.

The quotation from Psalm xcv. 7–11 is introduced as the words of the Holy Spirit, thus implying the divine authorship of the Psalm. The use of the present tense *saith*, to show that the Holy Spirit is still speaking, greatly increases the importance of the words and the danger of disobeying them. In the Hebrew *To day if ye will hear his voice* is a common way of expressing a wish and can, therefore, be rendered 'Oh, if ye would but hear His voice'; yet the RSV 'when you hear his voice' more exactly reproduces the sense, for, as Westcott remarks, 'in the old times the people fell away when the divine voice was still sounding in their ears.' All readers of the Epistle are reminded that 'to day' God is speaking in Someone greater than the prophets, greater than angels, greater than Moses; therefore He demands implicit obedience. When His voice is heard the heart should be responsive and not hardened. This exhortation may have been made at a time when other voices were asking them to support their brethren in the defence of country and temple. The 'heart' in Scripture is often equivalent to the mind, viewed as endowed with intelligence and affection. The revelation of God in His Son, and the grace behind it, should appeal greatly to the mind and heart of man; yet sometimes the ear hears the voice, but the mind does not appreciate the revelation nor does the heart respond. As this rejection of God's grace is man's own act it produces hardness of heart. The tense used in the Greek might suggest a single act of hardening; but this does not necessarily mean the final resistance to God's voice and grace. Each day God may speak, and each day He may be resisted; but He may also be accepted. Yet the constant resistance of the voice and the refusal of grace may produce a habit of resistance which cannot be broken, and the judicial sentence of God, which at last endorses this, is applied to that hardened heart.

In the original both *provocation* and *temptation* are proper names. In the LXX they are translations of the Hebrew words *Meribah* and *Massah*. The two illustrations given of the hardening of the heart are taken from the history of those who left Egypt under Moses. As one is found at the beginning of the wanderings (Ex. xvii. 1-7) and the other at the end (Nu. xiv. 1-13), the suggestion is that the hardening of the heart was a process which persisted for forty years.

Some modern commentators have suggested that the author

has made use of a tradition deduced from Psalm xcv that 'the days of Messiah' would be for a duration of forty years. It is much more likely, however, that the author saw a typical resemblance between the attitude of those Jews who for forty years saw the works of God in the wilderness, and the attitude of those Jews who for almost the same period had seen the works of God in Christ and in the early Church. The author may also have been influenced by our Lord's words in Luke xxi. 20, 21. The fact that in viii. 13 he mentions that the old system was about to vanish away shows that he perceived the judgment was about to fall, and he may have been guided to this pronouncement by our Lord's prediction that the temple and Jerusalem would be destroyed.

10. *Wherefore* is not found in the Psalm and is used here to clarify the connection. Because of their continued unbelief and because of their defiance of His goodness and works, God *was grieved with that generation*. The AV has softened the Hebrew which states that God was 'incensed' against that generation. A twofold statement is now made against them. Firstly, they were habitually wayward in their moral life; error was always in their hearts. Secondly, *they have not known my ways*, which is better expressed by the RV 'but they did not know my ways'. The phrase is not a continuation of the preceding clause but a statement of a further fact that, though God was grieved, they, for their part, did not acquire that knowledge of God's ways which would have saved them from God's final decision to exclude them from His rest.

11. *So I sware in my wrath* reflects the intensity and depth of God's displeasure. Later in the Epistle the author reminds us that 'it is a fearful thing to fall into the hands of the living God' (x. 31). The strong assertion *They shall not enter into my rest* referred originally to that rest which was associated with the possession of the promised land. (See additional note on 'Rest', p. 9.)

12. The words *take heed . . . lest* suggest deep anxiety lest the readers will not respond to the warning; they translate *blepete mē*, which occurs again in xii. 25, where it is followed by the subjunctive as in normal usage. Here, however, the phrase is followed by the future indicative which, according to J. H. Moulton, presumably makes the warning somewhat more instant. 'It marks the reality and urgency of the danger. Take heed! Perhaps there will be someone with an evil heart of unbelief.' It is not important whether the evil heart is the result of unbelief, as some commentators suggest, or unbelief the result of the evil heart, as is maintained by others. The author viewed any return to Judaism as an act of unfaithfulness towards Christ and unbelief towards God. He urges his readers to go the whole way, for apparently they had stopped short of embracing the true Christian faith. Judaism was indeed God-given, but having served its purpose it must of necessity give way to Christianity. To turn from the latter was to forsake Christ, and to forsake Christ was to reject God and His revelation in Christ. Such a rejection of Christianity meant that the rejector would have to face *the living God*, which means not 'the true God' but 'the living, powerful God', suggesting the certainty of retribution on unfaithfulness, for God cannot allow His declared will to be slighted with impunity.

13. Although *heautous* literally means 'yourselves', *exhort one another* is correct in this passage (as in Mk. x. 26), for the interdependence of the whole Christian body is in mind. *Exhort* is the word from which Paraclete, i.e. Comforter, is derived, and the exhortation must, therefore, have in it that element of comfort which will strengthen and encourage the believer each single day so that when a crisis arises he may be able to stand fast. As Calvin said, 'Unless our faith be now and then raised up, it will lie prostrate; unless it is warmed, it will be frozen; unless it be roused, it will grow torpid.' For the individual *To day* cannot exceed the period of his own life which is exceedingly brief; yet the use of the expression in this passage suggests a crisis, a time near at hand when 'To day' will be no longer applicable. It is the possibility of such a crisis which causes the author to plead with his readers to *exhort one another daily*.

Lest any of you relates the danger to the individual, who may *be hardened through the deceitfulness of sin*. Sin is almost personified here, as it is in Romans vii. It deceives the sinner, exaggerating the satisfaction that can be gained from sin, then blinds his mind to spiritual truth and also to the certainty of God's retribution. It is possible that sin had already deceived some of the readers by giving them a romantic faithfulness to the past and by blinding them to the dangers so clearly brought out in this Epistle.

14, 15. As the perfect tense is used, *we are made partakers of Christ* is better rendered 'we have become partakers'. They had not been partakers of Christ from the beginning, but the author assumes that, like himself, they had acquired this privilege and blessing by faith. Compare iv. 2 where the necessity of faith is mentioned. Mention of this experience of Christ is at once followed by the qualification *if we hold the beginning of our confidence stedfast unto the end*. The commencement of the Christian life is not sufficient, there must be a continuation and completion. Each day is important. Hence the repetition of the words from Psalm xcv in verse 15. The Greek word here translated *confidence, hupostasis*, is different from the word translated 'confidence' in verse 6. It denotes the 'sense of assurance' which comes from the realization that the revelation of God in Jesus Christ is true.

16. *For* is a connecting link between the last three verses of this chapter and those which have gone before. The AV construes the Greek *tines* as indefinite, *some*, but both the RV and RSV rightly take it as the interrogative 'who'. This is supported by its position, and corresponds better with the two interrogatives which follow. Thus in verses 16–18 three questions are asked and three answers in the form of questions given. Who were those who, when they heard the voice, provoked? Was it not all those who left Egypt? Was it not those who heard the message, experienced God's redemption and saw His works and yet did not believe? This was their sin of provocation; it continued for the whole period of forty years, and brought upon them the judgment of God even while they were on their way to the land of promise.

17, 18. The question has been asked whether Moses and Aaron, who died in the wilderness, came under this condemnation. Although both of these men may have sinned as individuals, they were not unbelievers, and no doubt there were others who were like-minded. They were very different from that large body of unbelievers who publicly resisted God, provoked Him for forty years and displayed an obstinacy of unbelief which brought upon them the anger and oath of God.

19. *So we see*, says the author, drawing the inevitable deduction from the facts found in Numbers xiv to which he has drawn attention, *they could not enter in because of unbelief.* God's grace had opened the way to rest, God's purpose was that some should enter, yet God's power alone enables the believer to accomplish this. But this power cannot operate in an evil heart of unbelief. Such a heart was found in the Israelites; it was found also at Nazareth where our Lord could do no mighty works. The warnings already given suggest that there was evidence of the evil heart in some of the readers. And since the same evil heart is found in many today, the warnings are still applicable.

c. The gospel of rest (iv. 1–13)

1. The unbelieving Israelites who perished did not nullify the promise that some should enter into God's rest, nor was the promise fulfilled when their children entered the promised land. The rest that these enjoyed was only a type of God's rest and, therefore, incomplete. The promise of God that some should enter His rest still remains, but in the light of what happened to those who left Egypt an exhortation to fear is given to the readers. This exhortation carries with it a suggestion that each reader should examine himself lest he be still not in the way which leads to that rest. The AV translation of *dokeo*, *seem*, can mean only that so great is the issue that any appearance of failure is something to fear. The RSV has 'be judged', which gives a better sense, for the knowledge of certain judgment is a greater reason for fear than any appearance of failure. MM translate *husterēkenai* (AV, *to come short*) by 'come late', 'are late', and some commentators have suggested that the author is trying to console those who despaired of being able to attain salvation because they were too late. But in the passive the Greek word sometimes has the meaning 'to come short of through one's own fault' as in Romans iii. 23, and this seems to be the meaning of the word here, although it cannot be ruled out that when some stand before God's throne of judgment they will realize that they are too late, that they have for ever missed their chance of God's rest.

2. The readers were partakers of this heavenly promise as well as of a heavenly calling, for the glad tidings of salvation (or 'rest') were preached to them as well as to their fathers in the wilderness. But the message which the Israelites heard from Moses was not perceived as God's, nor did the works of God which supported it reveal to them His ways, for these met with no faith in those who heard. Two different readings in the Greek, *sunkekerasmenos* and *sunkekerasmenous*, have given rise to the two different interpretations found in the AV and RV. If the former is correct, the sense of the passage is that the message which the Israelites heard did not meet with that responsive faith in the hearers which could make the good news effectual. On the other hand, if the RV has rendered the correct reading, then the passage can mean only that the word which they heard did not profit them because they were not united by faith with those who (truly) heard, i.e. with Moses, Joshua and Caleb, who not only heard but believed. The AV is simpler than the RV and the introduction of a faithful remnant, as Moffatt suggests, seems out of harmony with the rest of the passage.

3, 4. In contrast with those who through unbelief were excluded from God's rest there are those who have believed the message brought by Christ and, therefore, are entering into that rest, or 'are sure to enter in'. *If they shall enter into my rest* is a literal translation of the Greek which is simply an idiomatic use of a strong negative and, therefore, it should be translated 'they shall not enter' as in iii. 11. The same idiomatic use occurs in Mark viii. 12. If God is still warning the readers to fear lest, through unbelief, they do not enter His rest, it is obvious that the possibility of obtaining the rest is not past and gone but in fact still exists. It had been in existence since the creation-work of God was completed, and God rested from all His works. This rest of God, however, cannot mean complete inactivity, for the administration of the universe and the work of man's salvation must continue (cf. Jn. v. 17).

The indefinite mode of expression in verse 4 is not found elsewhere in the New Testament, but is common in Philo and the Rabbis. The *certain place* (RSV 'somewhere') is most probably Genesis ii. 2, though Exodus xx. 11 and xxxi. 17 may also have been in view.

5, 6. Since God's Word cannot be broken, the promise of rest still remains open (cf. verse 1). Because of disobedience, those who came out of Egypt at the Exodus and who received the promise of rest did not enter into it. It is true that the next generation entered Canaan, but the fact that the rest was offered again in the Psalm, even when the Israelites were in possession of the land, proves that 'the rest' cannot mean simply the earthly settlement which was secured under Joshua. But as God's purpose to bring some into His rest has not been fulfilled, a rest still remains open under the Christian dispensation.

7, 8. It is the Holy Spirit who has appointed a certain day during which men may enter this rest. It is the Holy Spirit who spoke in David, i.e. in the person of David, as He did in the prophets and in the Son (i. 1, 2). Some commentators make this expression equivalent to 'saying in the Book of Psalms which goes by the name of David'. This may be true, yet the lxx attributes this Psalm to David, and although this may be a later addition yet it is a very early one. In any case, as Nairne points out, the stress is not on the tradition of human authorship but on the Holy Spirit, who spoke in David to show that long after the divine sentence had fallen on the disobedient in the wilderness the rest was still available.

The great conqueror of Canaan, Joshua (*Jesus* is simply the Greek form of Joshua), gave the children of Israel a certain rest (Jos. xxi. 44, xxii. 4); but this did not fulfil the promise of God.

9. The change here from *katapausis*, which has been used throughout the Epistle for 'rest', to *sabbatismos*, 'sabbath rest', is very significant. The word is found only here in biblical Greek and the possibility exists that it may have been coined by the author. It echoes Genesis ii. 2. Rendall suggests that the use of the term in a spiritual sense, without comment or explanation, seems to point to a decay in the observance of the Jewish Sabbath amongst the Hebrew Christians. Moses and the law failed to give the people rest. The same to a large extent could be said of Joshua and the promised land. The old covenant had come to an end and a new covenant had been made. A new *people of God* through this new covenant had taken the place of the old. These were the believers who were entering into God's sabbath rest.

10. Some ancient and modern commentators take *he* to be Jesus Christ. Whereas it is quite true that Christ has ceased from His work of creation and His work of redemption, yet the reference can hardly be to Christ for the following reasons: (i) We seem to have here a universal proposition, as is brought out by the RSV which correctly translates 'for whoever enters God's rest'. (ii) Christ is never mentioned in the context, and His introduction here would not only be strange but out of harmony with the main purpose of the author, unless he intended the readers to understand that Christ has entered into rest, and that therefore all in Christ will be led into rest; this is possible but improbable. This verse elucidates the 'sabbath rest' of the previous verse; but the entrance could be at conversion or at death, for in both places 'rest' follows. The context suggests that the final rest is in mind. The writer has now mentioned three of the blessings connected with salvation— the restoration of the dominion which man lost at the fall (ii. 8, 9); deliverance not only from the fear of death but from the power of death, which were the result of the fall (ii. 14, 15); and the restoration of that rest which man lost through the fall (iii. 7–iv. 13). There may be some truth in the objection to the RSV translation that at the present there is little evidence of the restoration of these three blessings to man; yet the believer has by the eye of faith seen the Man Jesus as the conqueror of death through His resurrection, as the crowned King of the universe through His exaltation, and as resting from His creative and redemptive work by His position at the right hand of God. For the man without faith it can only be said 'Eye hath not seen, nor ear heard, neither have entered into the heart of man, the things which God hath prepared for them that love him.' But for the man with faith God has revealed them to him by His Spirit (see 1 Cor. ii. 9, 10).

11. The author exhorts his readers to be zealous, or strive eagerly to enter this rest *lest any man fall* into the same unbelief and disobedience as those in the wilderness and thus become, like them, an example to others of unbelief and disobedience.

12. The early Fathers commonly understood the *word of God* to mean the personal Word. They were probably influenced by John i. 1, 14, where the logos certainly refers to Jesus Christ, who is spoken of as God manifest in the flesh, and by Revelation xix. 13 where 'his name is called The Word of God'. Such a connection of 'the word' with Christ came through the identification of the word of God with God's activity, and God was active in Christ. Yet in our text it is not the personal Word of John i but the word which God speaks, i.e. the teaching or message of Holy Scripture, which brings a warning of the possibility of the exclusion of the unbeliever from His rest, and a promise that the believer is sure to enter. But it must not be assumed that the Word of God is a mere fixed and dead letter. On the contrary it is alive (*quick*) and *powerful*, for it is the Word of the living God who makes effective its warnings on the disobedient, and its promises on the believer. It penetrates into the deepest and most hidden parts of a man's life and dissects his lower animal life with its desires, interests and affections, from his higher spiritual life with its aspirations for spiritual communion with God, just as a two-edged sword cuts through *the joints and marrow* of a physical body. It does not look upon outward appearances but is skilled in judging *the thoughts* and intentions *of the heart*. Robertson likens this to 'The surgeon who carries a bright and powerful light for every dark crevice and a sharp knife for the removal of the pus revealed by the light'. Opinions about man's heart are numerous, yet through lack of knowledge they are imperfect. But God's Word does not lack this knowledge; therefore to know fully the human heart one must know God's Word.

13. There is a sudden transition from the penetrating power of God's Word to the omniscient God before whose eyes *all things are naked and opened* (RSV 'laid bare'). Whereas the meaning of *trachēlizō* in this passage seems clear enough the metaphor from which it is derived is obscure. Of the many suggestions two are worthy of consideration. The first associates it with a wrestler's grip on the neck (Gk. *trachēlos*) of an opponent, thus suggesting someone at the mercy of another. The second connects it with the sacrificial victim gripped by the neck to expose the throat. The former suggests the guilty sinner seeking to hide his face with shame at the exposure of all his guilt before God. The latter implies that no-one can ever hide himself from the all-searching eyes of God. The fact that we cannot hide from God and that He is the One *with whom we have to do* or 'with whom we have to reckon' means that we should believe His Word, obey His voice and seek His power in our lives, so that when we stand before the Judge we may not be ashamed, but be judged worthy, through a heart of faith, to enter His rest.

Additional note: 'Rest' (iv. 1-13)

There are various shades of meaning attached to the word 'rest'.

(i) Genesis ii. 2 speaks of *creation rest* (mentioned here in iv. 3, 4) when God rested 'from all his work which he had made'. That this rest did not mean inactivity is clear from 'My Father worketh hitherto (even until now), and I work' (Jn. v. 17). God rested from creative work but continues to uphold creation by His operative power and administrative rule. Furthermore, the Father and Son co-operate in the redemption of man and restoration of all things. This rest of creation is a type of redemption rest. It reminds the Christian of a work completed by Christ, who has entered into this rest, and that one day he will share in God's rest when his own work is finished on earth.

(ii) Deuteronomy i. 34–36, xii. 9; Joshua xxiii. 1 speak of *Canaan rest* which is referred to in the use made by our author of Psalm xcv quoted in iii. 7–11. It is very difficult, in the light of iv. 8 and 11, to believe that the Psalmist had only the rest of Canaan in mind. Yet if he had in mind a higher and spiritual rest, it cannot possibly mean the rest of heaven, for in that case it would mean that all who died in the wilderness were excluded from heaven. This exclusion would include Moses and Aaron. Yet the incident of the transfiguration shows that Moses appeared in glory (Lk. ix. 28–36). The rest of Canaan is a type of consecration rest, that is, of the rest which comes from a surrender of the mind, will and heart to God's power and influence which enables the believer to conquer sin. Joshua gave the children of Israel rest from their enemies but the Israelites in the wilderness through unbelief never entered into this rest. They never at any time had true and lasting fellowship with God.

(iii) A *sabbath rest* is mentioned in iv. 9 and in Exodus xx. 8–11 and both passages have been likened to celestial rest (cf. Rev. xiv. 13) 'that they may rest from their labours; and their works do follow them'. Others, like Calvin, have connected iv. 9 with the sabbath day which is a day of rest and gladness. Yet the verse seems primarily concerned with the present rather than with the future, with the believer's rest here, and with heaven only as its completing and culminating point. It seems better, therefore, to connect it with spiritual rest of the soul in fellowship with God which has come to pass through a definite personal contact with Jesus Christ (cf. Mt. xi. 28).

IV. THE MERCIFUL AND GREAT HIGH PRIEST (iv. 14–v. 10)

Reference has already been made to our merciful and faithful High Priest (ii. 17). His faithfulness the author has already discussed in iii. 1–6. He now deals with His gracious and sympathetic nature (iv. 14–16) and discusses the general qualifications of priesthood (v. 1–4) and how Christ satisfies these qualifications (v. 5–10).

a. Our gracious and sympathetic High Priest (iv. 14–16)

14. The emphatic nature of the statement *we have a great high priest* suggests that some Jews were claiming that there was in

Christianity no priesthood like the Aaronic. The author not only claims that such a High Priest does in fact exist, but by his use of *great* asserts that He is a person of high distinction and power and, therefore, greater than Aaron. His ministry also excels the Aaronic for it takes place not in the holy place of the tabernacle but in the presence of God Himself, for Jesus has *passed into* (through) *the heavens*. Jewish tradition of this period spoke of seven heavens, but Paul in 2 Corinthians xii. 2 mentions only three. Yet Ephesians iv. 10 refers to 'all the heavens' (RSV). No more is meant here than that the exaltation of Christ, already referred to in i. 3 and ii. 9, was from the lower world (the earth) through the middle world (the heavens) to the higher world (the place of God's presence). In a similar way the high priest on the day of atonement passed from the courts of the tabernacle through the holy place into the holy of holies. The bringing together of the human and divine natures by use of the phrase *Jesus the Son of God* was to encourage the readers to *hold fast* their confession. The human nature gave the assurance of sympathy, and the divine the confidence of strength. These characteristics were necessary to sustain those who through weakness were in danger of denying their declaration of acceptance, not only of Christ as High Priest but of the whole Christian faith.

15. *Infirmities* or weaknesses do not necessarily refer to sin here, nor should they be limited to sufferings; they cover all the frailties of human nature. In the New Testament the word *sunpathein*, to sympathize, is found only here and in x. 34 (cf. 1 Pet. iii. 8). A. T. Robertson suggests that it is a late compound verb from the late adjective *sunpathos* which is derived from *sunpascho* (to suffer with). The AV, in beautiful phraseology, adopts this last meaning, suggesting that our great High Priest not only sympathizes with those who suffer the things which He has suffered, but also that He suffers when His children suffer. This would have been more naturally expressed by the use of *sunpascho*. Yet the words, 'Saul, Saul, why persecutest thou me?' (Acts ix. 4), and Augustine's comment, 'it was the head in heaven crying out on behalf of the members who were still on earth', convey something of the meaning of our text as translated in the AV.

When Christ took upon Himself human nature He became subject to all its limitations and trials. There is, however, one exception: He has no experimental knowledge of sin. By the introduction of *yet* into the text the AV takes *without sin* to mean that though our Lord was tempted with all the temptations which men have to face He yielded to none of them. Temptations arise in many cases as a direct sinful connection with, or as a result of, previous sin. Christ, though made in the likeness of sinful flesh, did not possess sinful flesh. Even with regard to this Christ could say, 'the prince of this world cometh, and hath nothing in me' (Jn. xiv. 30). Therefore, it has been argued that the temptations or trials which our Lord had to endure were apart from those associated with previous sin or sinful connection. That there is truth in this latter suggestion few will deny, but it is open to the misconception of implying that it was impossible for Jesus to sin, and this would destroy the whole meaning of temptation in the life of Christ.

16. As the word *come* is used frequently both in the LXX and in this Epistle of the sinner's approach to God for worship, it is legitimate to maintain that the guilty sinner should always draw near to God as a worshipper. Then the use of the present tense suggests that the *time of need* will frequently arise; therefore the believer must come regularly to the *throne of grace*— his approach should become a daily spiritual exercise. Being guilty, and having no merits of his own, his fundamental need is mercy; but through the weakness of the flesh, even after receiving mercy, he has no hope of conquering sin, therefore he needs grace. Knox's translation 'win that grace' is somewhat unfortunate, as it might suggest a reward for human merit which would be quite contrary to what the author had in mind. He must *come boldly* (RSV 'with confidence') to *the throne of*

grace, which does not mean 'Christ' as some commentators suggest, nor does it typify the mercy-seat above the ark (Ex. xxv.
21) over which the shekinah, or the revelation of glory, was
displayed. It is simply the throne of God where a crucified,
risen and glorified Saviour sits. It is called a 'throne of grace'
in contrast to the 'throne of judgment' which displays the awful
majesty of God; and the Christian should come to it regularly
and with confidence.

b. The qualifications of a true priest (v. 1–4)

Two conditions given as essential for a valid priesthood are a
sympathetic human nature (1–3) and divine appointment (4).

1. Three characteristics associated with the Jewish priesthood are here briefly mentioned. First, he must be *taken from
among men* (RSV 'chosen from among men', which is better).
Second, the purpose for which he is chosen is to act *for men in
things pertaining to God*, i.e. in their relations with God. Third,
to fulfil this purpose he has to *offer both gifts and sacrifices for sins*.
Gifts in this passage most probably signifies inanimate 'offerings and oblations', and *sacrifices* would seem to refer to the
offering of animate things, viz. slain beasts. In the Old Testament, however, this distinction does not always hold good (cf.
Gn. iv. 3, 5, iv. 4; Lv. i. 2, 3, 10), but where both words are
used together it would appear to do so.

2, 3. Furthermore, the high priest must be one *who can have
compassion* (RV, 'who can bear gently'). The Greek word so
translated, *metriopathein*, is a philosophical term which expresses the feeling of moderation which lies between apathy,
or 'lack of feeling', and undue excitement. There should be no
lack of feeling on the part of the high priest for those who have
fallen into error and sin, nor should he be unduly disturbed,
otherwise he may fail to bear gently with them. This feeling of
moderation should arise naturally from a knowledge of his
own sinful weaknesses, for high priests are *compassed with in-*

firmity just as other men are. They are encircled by sinful weakness as by a chain. In consequence, as the ritual for the day of atonement makes clear, the high priest, being recognized as guilty, has to make an atonement for himself before he can make atonement for others. Therefore it is necessary for him to avoid undue severity, for he is under the same condemnation; yet, as God's representative, he cannot be too lenient, for God never overlooks sin.

4. A fifth characteristic of the priesthood is now stated. The high priest does not take office of himself but is chosen and appointed by God. This refers to the divine ideal of priesthood, for history furnishes us with a number of instances of persons who acquired the office by force or fraud. As Westcott rightly points out, 'the notoriousness of the high priestly corruption at the time could not fail to give point to the language of the Epistle'.

c. The validity of Christ's priesthood (v. 5–10)

Our Lord was invested with the high priesthood according to the conditions already stated. His incarnation endowed Him with human nature and His experience of temptation with the feeling of sympathy. He was divinely appointed (5, 6) and successfully discharged the functions of His priesthood (7–10).

5, 6. The truth that *Christ glorified not himself* is illustrated by His own words. 'If I honour myself, my honour is nothing: it is my Father that honoureth me' (Jn. viii. 54). The explanatory infinitive *to be made* shows that the glory of being a high priest was not self-assumed. He to whom the appointment belonged bestowed upon Christ the title, function and dignity of this priesthood.

It was the voice of God which proclaimed to Christ *Thou art my Son, to day have I begotten thee* (see Ps. ii. 7). It was the same voice which said *Thou art a priest for ever after the order of Melchisedec* (see Ps. cx. 4). The former reference suggests

Christ's fitness for such an office, and the latter quotation is proof that His appointment was by the irrevocable oath of God. It is not necessary to maintain that *for ever* makes the priesthood as eternal as Sonship. Such a claim cannot be divorced from the insoluble origin of sin, for the priesthood is related to sin. Christ's priesthood could not begin earlier than His incarnation, though the declaration that He was to be a *priest . . . after the order of Melchisedec* is clearly as old as Psalm cx. 4. Moffatt points out that in the strict sense of the term there was no succession of Melchisedec priests. Even so, in this passage the Greek word *taxis* can only mean 'priestly office' or 'order'. A full discussion of Melchisedec appears in chapter vii, but according to his usual style the author prepares the way for that discussion by the introduction of the name here.

7. Although the High Priest of their confession is in glory, yet *in the days of his flesh*, i.e. in His incarnate life on earth, He had personal trials of suffering which gave Him the necessary experience to be gracious and sympathetic. What greater proof of these sufferings could be given than the experience in the Garden of Gethsemane, which is now described with such vividness, solemnity and pathos? *With strong crying and tears* indicates the intensity of these sufferings, *prayers* the vehement cry of one in desperate need, while *supplications* describes 'the supplication of one in need of protection or help in some overwhelming calamity' (Westcott). (See further, Additional Note, p. 99.)

And was heard in that he feared may mean that our Lord was heard on account of His pious reverence to God. This has been objected to on the grounds that if the author had meant this he would have used the preposition *dia* with the accusative. But the preposition *apo* used here also has a causal sense, both in Classical and Hellenistic Greek. On the other hand it could mean that the object of Christ's fear was all the evils to which He was exposed, which brought upon Him the awful judgment of God, and the sense of desertion by God; but He was not overwhelmed by them. Although this latter view is supported by Calvin, the former is to be preferred.

8. In verse 7 the humanity and humiliation of Christ are vividly portrayed; but now, in the words *Though he were a Son*, stress is laid upon the quality of His sonship. Even though He was the eternal Son, and had no need of obedience or of suffering, *yet learned he obedience by the things which he suffered.* *Learned . . . obedience* does not mean that previously He was rebellious and disobedient, for such an idea cannot be applied to the Son. Griffith Thomas has rightly said 'This is the difference between innocency and virtue. Innocency is life untested, while virtue is innocency tested and triumphant'.[1] The Son had always possessed the disposition of obedience, but for Him to possess the virtue of obedience, testing was necessary. Classical writers consistently point out that suffering brought experimental knowledge but not necessarily obedience. Our Lord acquired by means of suffering the experimental knowledge of obedience, for the suffering He endured was according to the Father's will.

9. The fitness of Jesus for His work is now stressed, for *teleiōtheis*, translated *made perfect*, means 'made mature' or 'complete'. In the first place, Jesus was 'complete' in having obtained every necessary qualification for the office of priesthood. He had the authority and calling of His Father; He became the possessor of human nature and sympathy; He surrendered His will to the obedience and will of God; and He offered on the cross the perfect sacrifice. In the second place, He was 'complete' in the sense that He was crowned with glory by His exaltation to the right hand of God. Thus He became fit to become *the author of eternal salvation*, for in His character as High Priest He offered Himself as an expiatory sacrifice for our sins and, therefore, He became through this expiatory sacrifice the Saviour of man.

[1] *Let us go on*, p. 62.

The writer adds, however, a qualifying clause, pointing out that Christ is the author of eternal salvation only *unto all them that obey him*, thus leaving no room for 'universal salvation'. Obedience necessarily presupposes a revelation of the will of the person to be obeyed, and for its wider meaning cf. x. 7 ff. Here the writer is concerned with the revealed will of God for man and 'obedience' to this will, but the expression *them that obey him* is not fundamentally different from 'we which have believed' in iv. 3.

10. To be the cause and mediator of eternal salvation Christ must be the possessor of high priestly dignity, therefore when He ascended on high He was named by God *an high priest after the order of Melchisedec*. This pronouncement by God meant that the Aaronic priesthood had been passed by, for Christ was a priest not of law but of promise. The original dispensation was wider than Judaism under the law, and the Christian dispensation is the full expansion of the original economy rather than of the later.

Additional Note on v. 7

The Greek preposition *ek* translated *from* in the phrase *to save him from death* can also mean 'out of'. If 'out of' is adopted, the meaning of the phrase would be to bring Him safe through death to a new life, a clear reference to Christ's resurrection. If 'from' is adopted, then it would appear that Jesus prayed to be preserved from death, either in the Garden as some suggest, or on the cross. This last interpretation should be ruled out for two reasons: Christ did suffer the death of the cross; and His prayer in the Garden was answered. We are left, then, with the following alternatives: Did Christ pray to be saved 'out of' the death of the cross? or did He pray to be saved 'from' dying in the Garden?

If the prayer which Christ offered *with strong crying and tears* was a prayer to be saved 'out of' death, it cannot easily be reconciled with another request made in the Garden—'Father, if thou be willing, remove this cup from me' (Lk. xxii. 42). In the first place, our Lord knew that man's only hope of salvation lay in His death on the cross, and this was the way ordained by God. He was willing to go this way, and prayed, according to this interpretation, that He might safely be brought through it to the resurrection. It seems strange, then, that He should pray almost in the same breath that 'this cup', which can only mean the cup of death, should pass from Him. It is true that He was willing to submit to the Father's will, but why should He pray that the cup of death should pass from Him, when shortly before He had not only prayed a different prayer but had rejected the idea that He should be saved from 'this hour' (cf. Jn. xii. 27)? The 'hour' can mean only the great crisis of His life, and from this He says He will not shrink; yet apparently He does shrink from it shortly afterwards. Moreover, Christ in the upper room shortly before He went into the Garden spoke of His death and resurrection, and, as recorded in Mark xiv. 28, made an appointment with His disciples to meet Him in Galilee after the resurrection, yet in an incredibly short space of time He is found, if this interpretation is correct, not only praying to be saved from the 'cup of death' but also to be saved 'out of' death.

In support of the second interpretation, the everyday meaning of the phrase is 'to save from dying', i.e., to deliver from physical death so that it is escaped. In Matthew xxvi. 38 our Lord said, 'My soul is exceeding sorrowful, even unto death.' R. A. Knox translates this, 'My soul is ready to die with sorrow . . .' We have already seen that *prayers and supplications* means 'the vehement cry of one in desperate need', and 'the supplication of one in need of protection or help in some overwhelming calamity'. If Christ had died in the Garden, no greater calamity could possibly have fallen on mankind. Immediately after our Lord had spoken about this condition of His soul, He prayed for the cup to pass from Him and 'was heard'. Luke records: 'there appeared an angel unto him from heaven, strengthening him' (xxii. 43). The great agony of the

Saviour of the world will ever remain a mystery to us in this life, and so will various other aspects of His suffering. No-one can, therefore, afford to be dogmatic concerning the meaning of this very difficult phrase.

V. SPIRITUAL PROGRESS (v. 11–vi. 20)

The writer had many fundamental matters to speak about, but these were only for full-grown Christians. Unfortunately his readers were still in their infancy (v. 11–14). Nevertheless he exhorts them to advance to manhood (vi. 1–3) and then gives one of the most solemn warnings in the New Testament (vi. 4–8).

a. Spiritual infancy (v. 11–14)

11. The subject of Christ's priesthood was one of considerable difficulty but it was certainly not beyond explanation, nor was it beyond the writer's ability to explain it, but his readers had become confused and limited in their minds through apathy and mental listlessness. They had become *dull of hearing*, which was a common Greek ethical term for a sluggish intelligence.

12. This habit of spiritual apathy towards the things of God not only hinders progress but produces retrogression. It is impossible for the mind to stand still when dealing with the utterances of God. If the dark things do not become plain then the plain things will become dark. This was the predicament of the readers of this Epistle. They ought to have been teachers but their low spiritual state revealed their lack of perception of *the first principles of the oracles of God* and their need of someone to teach them again the elementary truths of the revelation of God. The Greek word *logion*, here rendered *oracle*, originally meant a 'brief, condensed, divine saying'. It is quite common in the Old Testament and in Philo, who uses it in connection with the prophecies and the Ten Commandments. It is used by Luke in Acts vii. 38 of the revelation re-

ceived by Moses, and by Paul in Romans iii. 2 of the law given
from Sinai, and more especially of God's promises to the Jews
about the Messiah. In 1 Peter iv. 11 'oracles of God' seems to
be used in a wider sense. It is difficult, therefore, to decide
whether the phrase here refers to Judaism or to the Christian
revelation, but the weight of evidence and the context seem in
favour of Judaism. Rideout says, 'the period of infancy is
Judaism and the period of manhood is Christianity'.

13. Both *milk* and *strong meat* are nourishment divinely provided—the former for babes and the latter for mature Christians. The readers, it would appear, had drifted into the position of the uninitiated, and had become *unskilful in the word of
righteousness. Dikaiosunē, righteousness,* is used in Romans and
Galatians with an almost uniform reference to justification,
and it is possible that this is its meaning here. Yet it may be
used in a wider sense and refer to Christian truth in general, or
to the gospel. The readers had not risen above the elementary
truth of the gospel and, therefore, were inexperienced *in the
word* or doctrine of the Christian faith. This verse lends little
support to the theory of E. F. Scott that the author was communicating a Christian 'gnosis' to a select group of disciples
to give them a truer and deeper conception of Christianity.

14. They who *are of full age* have reached an advanced stage
of spiritual understanding. They are mature or full grown in
the deep mysteries of the Word of God. This condition is not
gained by apathy or by slothfulness, for there is no room in the
Christian life for mental laziness. It is gained by the regular
exercise of the spiritual faculties in the Word of God and in
the doctrines of the Christian faith, for there is no easy way to
spiritual maturity. From this position those of *full age* can
discern both good and evil; they have an exact, or right,
judgment in all things. When different viewpoints are placed
before them they can at once distinguish the good from the
evil, the right from the wrong. As E. F. Scott finely says,

'Religion is something different from mere strenuous thinking on the great religious questions, yet it still remains true that faith and knowledge are inseparable, and that both grow stronger as they react on one another. More often than we know, the failure of a religion as a moral power is due to no other cause than intellectual sloth.'

b. The need to 'go on' (vi. 1-3)

It seems clear that the readers had linked themselves to some part of the Christian Church and had made some confession of the Christian faith, but no progress had been made. They had moved away from Judaism but had not proceeded far enough in Christianity. They had not advanced beyond the elementary truths of repentance, faith, baptisms (ablutions), laying on of hands, the resurrection of the dead, and eternal judgment. These doctrines were equally prominent in Judaism, and it is highly probable that the readers differed little from other Jews. The writer, realizing that while they were in this condition they were in danger of turning back, urges them to go on. v. 12 may imply that they should examine again the oracles of Judaism and compare them with the principles of Christianity. This should provide them with the right antidote to intellectual sloth and also help them towards a true spiritual grasp of the deeper truths of the new revelation in Christ. Nairne may be right, therefore, when he says the readers must needs learn again the Jewish elements of their faith in order to decide whether or no this new faith contains anything better than the old.

1, 2. An exhortation is now given urging the readers to move away from spiritual infancy and to go forward to spiritual maturity. Firstly, they must 'leave behind' or 'let go' *the principles of the doctrine of Christ*. A literal rendering of this last phrase, 'leaving behind the word of the beginning of Christ', when compared with the literal meaning of v. 12, 'the rudiments of the beginning of the oracles of God', shows that the sense is almost the same. If they are to reach spiritual maturity they must break away from Judaism. Unless this takes place no progress can be made towards a deeper and fuller Christian life. Secondly, they must *go on*, or 'move on', *unto perfection*. Personal effort is not the main theme here, for the idea is of a Christian yielding his life into the hands of Jesus Christ that he may be borne on, along with others, unto perfection. (Compare i. 3 where the same verb is used of the Son bearing all things forward to the consummation.)

The metaphorical use of *foundation* was quite common. Here it refers to elementary truths and thus stands in antithesis to maturity. The writer deprecates the idea that such a foundation, which consists of three fundamental pairs of elementary truths, can be laid afresh. The first pair, *repentance* and *faith*, refers to man's relation to God, for repentance in the New Testament means a change of attitude, spiritual and moral, towards God, which results in a movement from sin towards God. Here what is to be moved away from is described as *dead works*, by which is probably meant a reliance upon the ineffective Levitical sacrifices, though, as ix. 14 shows, the expression might mean 'sinful works' or 'guilty actions'. In the latter case they are called *dead works* because they produce death (cf. Romans vi. 23, 'the wages of sin is death'), or because they are the works of men who are 'dead in trespasses and sins' (Eph. ii. 1). Repentance alone is not sufficient to bring a man into a direct relationship with God; *faith toward God* or, rather, 'faith upon God' must be added. Moulton says, 'The Hebrew doctrine of faith connected itself closely with a cardinal passage of prophecy (Hab. ii. 4), "the just shall live by his faith".' The Christian doctrine does likewise (cf. Rom. i. 17 and Gal. iii. 11).

The second pair, *baptisms* and *laying on of hands*, deals with the individual's relation to the Church, whether the Church in the Old Testament or in the New. Baptism, whether in Judaism or in Christianity, is a symbolic act of cleansing or of the putting away of sin and the reception of a new spiritual life. The laying on of hands is a symbolic act denoting the communication of a gift through the prayer of the person who lays his hands upon another. In the New Testament it symbolizes the power of the Holy Spirit coming into the life of the person who through repentance and faith has embraced Christianity. Whether the phrase *doctrine of baptisms* refers to Christian baptism or not is not easy to decide. Baptism in the singular is always used of the latter, but here the plural of *baptisms* is used, and the RSV translates this phrase 'with instruction about ablutions'. In Mark vii. 8 and Hebrews ix. 10, the only other places where *baptismos* occurs, it denotes 'washings'. In some ancient MSS *baptismos* is inserted in Colossians ii. 12, where it would refer to Christian baptism, but this reading is probably inferior. Those who insist that the reference in our text is to Christian baptism maintain that the plural is used to distinguish it from the baptism of John and the ceremonial washings under the law. Before a man was accepted and acknowledged as a Christian by baptism it is supposed that he was instructed in the meaning of baptism, and if a Hebrew, in the difference between this baptism and the baptism under Judaism. Yet this does not seem to have taken place with those who were baptized in the early chapters of Acts, although some instruction was given later concerning the baptism of John and Christian baptism. The weight of evidence appears to be against Christian baptism.

The third pair of elementary truths is related to the future life. Both the *resurrection* and *eternal judgment* are eschatological doctrines found in the doctrinal system of orthodox Judaism (cf. Dn. vii. 9, 10, xii. 2; 2 Macc. vii; Lk. xx. 37, 38; Acts xxiii. 8). These six fundamentals originally found in Judaism were adopted later by the Christian Church.

3. The author, as some suggest, may simply mean by *this will we do* that on another occasion, if the way is open, he will teach those fundamental principles again, but for the present he must leave them to teach the deeper truths. Yet it hardly seems reasonable to give the more advanced teaching first and then to follow with what is elementary. It is better to believe that the author is not prepared to lay this foundation again, for it was imperative that he should proceed to the deeper truths of the Christian faith regardless of what the readers may do. By this action he most probably hoped that he would turn his readers from spiritual childhood to spiritual maturity. Yet a qualifying phrase *if God permit* is added, for every plan must be subordinated to the will of God.

c. The third warning (vi. 4–8)

4. As *therefore* in verse 1 links vi. 1–3 with v. 11–14 so *for* links verses 4–8 with these two former passages. The change of pronoun from 'we' to *those, they* and *them* suggests that these persons are different from the readers, and the phrase *if they shall fall away* is strongly in favour of this being a hypothetical case. The experience of *those who were once enlightened* must have happened at a certain time in the past, for the meaning here is a once and for all experience. Souter refers it to those who 'had experience of God's grace in conversion'. It could mean this, but the context does not necessarily suggest it. Some of the Fathers have associated this enlightenment with baptism and called the baptized person 'enlightened'; but there is little or no evidence to suggest that such a mode of expression was in use in the apostolic age. In the Old Testament the word sometimes bears the meaning 'instructed', which may be the meaning here. The persons concerned may have been instructed in the principles of Christianity.

Both Calvin and Owen reject the idea that *tasted of the heavenly gift* means 'experienced'; but in the light of ii. 9 and taking into account Psalm xxxiv. 8–10 ('O taste and see that the Lord is good'), which was most probably in the mind of the writer, it seems that the persons so described had an actual experience of the heavenly gift. This gift has been variously taken to mean the Holy Spirit, the forgiveness of sins, the gift of redemption, and the gift of grace. Support for all these can be found from other parts of Scripture, but it seems better to refer it to Jesus Christ who more than once claimed to have come down from heaven (cf. Jn. iii. 13, 31, 32, vi. 32, 35). *Tasted of the heavenly gift* could then refer to those who, through repentance and faith, have had a definite spiritual experience of Jesus Christ. The Jewish people, however, had an experience of the *heavenly gift* which was different from the spiritual experience just mentioned, and the writer may have had no more than this in mind.

Partakers of the Holy Ghost can refer only to the gifts, operations and influences of the Holy Spirit. Such activities of the third Person of the Trinity can lead to the new birth, but the creative work of the Holy Spirit is not the main thought here. The spiritual experience of the heavenly gift may be followed by spiritual experiences of the Holy Spirit which set their seal upon the hearts of those individuals who have experienced this gift of grace. On the other hand, it is possible that no more is meant than those experiences of the gifts, operations and influences of the Holy Spirit which had been experienced by all the Jewish people.

5. In verse 4 the Greek word for 'taste' is followed by the genitive but here by the accusative as in John ii. 9. Some have sought to make a distinction and translate 'tasted that the word of God is good'; but this seems unnecessary. Calvin denies that 'taste' means a real participation of *the good word of God*, and contrasts *kalon, good*, with the severity of the Mosaic law. That the writer was making a contrast between the good word of God and the severity of the law is very doubtful, and the words seem clearly to suggest that these persons had grasped the worth of the message of God.

The powers of the world to come are usually connected with the supernatural gifts associated with the messianic age and vividly displayed at Pentecost. The phrase may refer, however, to the future, i.e. to the resurrection of the body, the solemnities of judgment and the blessedness of everlasting life. In this case the powers operating in the life of the believer would be the presence of the Holy Spirit giving victory over sin, the assurance of salvation and a new life of blessedness. On the other hand, the words may simply refer to Christ's miracles experienced by the Jewish people. Referring to these miracles Alan Richardson says, 'Because they are the works of Christ, those who have witnessed them have already tasted the *dunameis (powers)* of the age to come (Heb. vi. 5).'[1]

6. The magnitude of the guilt of those who fall away can be seen only in the light of their great spiritual experiences. The writer by the use of the phrase *if they shall fall away* does not say that the readers or anyone else had fallen away. He is putting forward a hypothetical case as the RSV translation, 'if they then commit apostasy', suggests. If it were possible for them after their great experiences to reject completely and finally the grace of God found in the great work of Christ they would be guilty of committing 'the unforgivable sin', and it would be impossible *to renew them again unto repentance*. There is no suggestion in the context that the sin against the Holy Spirit, which Jesus regarded as unpardonable, and the mysterious 'sin unto death' (cf. 1 Jn. v. 16) is ever committed by true Christians. Moffatt maintains, 'The usage in Wisdom vi. 9, xii. 2 paves the way for this sense of deliberate renunciation of the Christian God, which is equivalent to "sin wilfully" in x. 26.' There is an important difference, however, for the writer of Wisdom gives little hint that those who fall away had anything like the experiences envisaged in Hebrews. In the first passage he has in mind the rulers of the earth who have not always been renowned for great spiritual experiences. In the second he is showing that the purpose was educative and such an object is far removed from the impossibility of repentance mentioned in Hebrews. In Classical Greek *anastauroun* does not mean to *crucify afresh* but simply to raise on the cross, i.e. 'to crucify'. The use of the dative case *to themselves* implies

[1] *An Introduction to the Theology of the New Testament*, p. 98.

that they are involved in the guilt of the crucifixion and, furthermore, they expose our Lord to the reproach and scorn of the world.

7, 8. An illustration from nature is now discussed to show the unnaturalness of those who fall away and the reasonableness of God's judgment—the impossibility of a renewed repentance. Here are two pieces of ground subject to the same favourable conditions. One responds to these conditions and brings forth fruit; but the other does not and remains unfruitful. The fruitful ground which *bringeth forth herbs* and *receiveth blessing from God* is a type of the true and mature Christian whose fruitfulness honours the blessings which God has showered upon him like rain upon the ground. Here the writer seems to have been influenced by Genesis i. 11, 12 where the earth is commanded by God to bring forth the herb of grass, and when it does so it receives God's approval. The unfruitful ground when put to the test shows itself unworthy of those blessings which God has showered upon it, for it *beareth thorns and briers*. It is a type of those who have received all the blessings and privileges mentioned in verses 4–6 and yet prove themselves unworthy. In this, the writer has been influenced by Genesis iii. 17–19 where, because of man's fall, the earth, which received a curse, was to bring forth thorns and thistles. The context does not favour the suggestion that the piece of ground should be burnt by man in order to improve it, nor does it favour the viewpoint of Chrysostom and others that *nigh unto cursing* is a sign of mercy. The whole paragraph suggests final destruction; and as Moffatt rightly says, 'there is no thought of mildness in the term *eggus* (near), it being used as in viii. 13 of imminent doom, which is only a matter of time.'

Additional Note on vi. 4–8

The difficulty of interpretation of one of the severest warnings given in Scripture cannot be exaggerated. This part of holy Scripture must be interpreted in the light of other parts of holy Scripture, and one part should not contradict another. The change of pronoun from *we* to *those, they* and *them* and then a return to *we* rules out the idea that the *readers* had fallen away. There are at least three possible interpretations worthy of serious attention.

1. The *Saved and Lost* theory. There are those who state that a Christian can be saved and yet lost through deliberate apostasy. Such expositors interpret these verses on this assumption. Although this appears simple enough, it is not without difficulties. First, there is little scriptural support for such a point of view. There are not more than five or six portions of Scripture in the New Testament which can really be quoted in its favour, yet each one of these passages is capable of another and, possibly, a better interpretation. Such passages are Matthew xxiv. 13; Mark iii. 29; Luke ix. 62; Hebrews x. 26; 1 John v. 16. Secondly, this view conflicts with many other passages which definitely teach the eternal security of those who are in Christ (e.g. Jn. v. 24, vi. 37; Jn. x. 28–30; Rom. viii. 1; Heb. viii. 12, etc.). Thirdly, such a possibility of falling away from grace as is suggested in this passage involves the impossibility of repentance, and this must mean for ever.

2. The *Non-Christian* theory. There are others who uphold that there is no mention in this passage of the new birth by God's Holy Spirit, nor is there any suggestion of faith in the hearts of the persons in question. The experiences mentioned fall short of real saving grace and can be illustrated by the seed which fell on rocky ground, or by the life of Judas Iscariot. Griffith Thomas rejects this point of view and says of the four statements mentioned in vi. 4–6 that 'they clearly imply a real and definite spiritual experience. It does not seem possible to interpret these phrases of illumination only of light rather than life.' On the other hand, Calvin, John Owen and many others maintain that they show that it is dangerously possible for a man to possess and to experience very much that is Christian without being in truth a new creature.

3. The *Hypothetical* theory. Others maintain that the writer

is dealing with supposition and not with fact, so that he may correct wrong ideas. If such a falling away could happen, he is saying, it would be impossible to renew them again unto repentance unless Christ died a second time, which is unthinkable. 'The case', says Westcott, 'is hypothetical. There is nothing to show that the conditions of fatal apostasy had been fulfilled: still less that they had been fulfilled in the case of any of those addressed. Indeed the contrary is assumed (verse 9 ff.).' Manson takes a similar view when he says, 'It would appear, then, that the catastrophe predicted . . . was hypothetical rather than real.' This theory has much in its favour and little against it. It in no way contradicts other passages of Scripture, neither is it in conflict with the doctrine of the perseverance of the saints.

d. Comfort and hope founded upon God's promise (vi. 9–20)

9. After one of the severest warnings given in holy Scripture the author shows by his use of *beloved* that he did not intend to leave his readers in blank despair. Firstly, his attitude, though inspired by love, rests upon his belief that 'in Christ' justice is always tempered by mercy and grace. By the use of a literary plural, *we are persuaded*, he expresses his conviction that his readers are genuine and that *better things* would come from them whatever may be his views about their present standard of Christianity. The use of the plural, *ta kreittona, better things*, suggests a fruitful spiritual life in contrast to a life bringing forth thorns and briers, and a destiny of eternal blessedness in contrast to the curse and perdition.

10. Secondly, his confidence rests upon the righteousness of God and the good deeds of his readers in the past. It was the grace and blessing of God which produced the good deeds, and not the good deeds the grace and blessing. Yet the manifestation of the good deeds is the evidence of the grace and blessing. Therefore any idea of merit must be ruled out. Most probably the words *labour of* were introduced into this passage in the later MSS through the influence of 1 Thessalonians i. 3 and should be omitted. If they are retained, the meaning would be that God would not forget their valuable *work* in ministering to the saints, nor their *labour of love* which they had shown towards His name, possibly in their open confession of the Christian faith. If they are omitted, then love must be the principle which brought into being that *work* or outward act of ministering to the saints. The intense longing of the author suggests that their acts of mercy were not so prominent as they had been in the past, and that there was still need for them to advance in these as well as in the deeper truths of the gospel.

11, 12. In v. 11 the danger to spiritual growth came from their sluggish intellects; from the same sluggishness came a further danger, lack of assurance in Christian *hope*. The way out of this danger was to throw off their spiritual indolence and become *followers* (or 'imitators', which is better) of the great heroes of the faith, whose victorious acts and patient endurance are given in chapter xi. These all obtained the promised inheritance of God and by similar faith and long-suffering the readers also would obtain *the promises*.

13. Abraham, the father of the faithful, is chosen as the great example of faith and perseverance. The oath referred to is found in Genesis xxii. 16, where the final promise of the Lord, which confirms all former promises, is given to Abraham. This oath is mentioned in Luke i. 73, but the context suggests that Zecharias was thinking rather of the last clause of Genesis xxii. 17, which deals with victory over Israel's enemies. In our passage, it is Abraham's victorious faith, his belief in God's declaration, and his perseverance until he obtained the promise which are in mind. God's oath was added to His word to give fuller assurance of its certainty and fulfilment, although God's word should be sufficient. In the Jewish treatise *Bera-*

choth (32.1), Moses is introduced as saying to God 'Hadst Thou sworn by Heaven and earth I should have said, even as Heaven and earth shall perish, so too Thine oath shall perish. But now Thou hast sworn by Thy great name, which lives and lasts for ever, so shall Thine oath last for ever and ever.'

14. The construction *blessing I will bless thee, . . . multiply thee* is a Hebraism and simply means 'I will greatly bless thee, and greatly multiply thee.' Vaughan remarks that with God benediction and benefaction are one.

15. *He obtained the promise* may refer to the giving of the promise or to the fulfilment of it. In favour of the former is xi. 39 which says that the faithful men of old 'received not the promise'; but this refers to a future and wider hope than that contained here. In favour of the latter is the giving back alive of Isaac, and the birth of Jacob and Esau; for in these events, though the promise was not fulfilled, it was on its way to fulfilment. Yet it was impossible for Abraham to see completely fulfilled such promises as those given in Genesis xxii. 17 and 18, for they contained two different prophecies. The first makes clear that his seed would be multiplied, and the second that all the nations of the world would be blessed. This latter statement could be accomplished only through the incarnation of Christ and His redemptive work on the cross.

16. The justification for, and the meaning and purpose of, the divine oath given in verses 16–18 is introduced by *for*. It is generally agreed that *men verily swear by the greater*, i.e. 'by God', for *tou meizonos* is most probably masculine and not neuter as some suggest. As God cannot swear by a greater, His oath is based upon His own great name. Now this *oath*, like the oaths of men, has the binding force of a legal guarantee, for *eis bebaiōsin, for confirmation,* bears such a meaning. According to Deissmann it is always used in a technical sense in the papyri. The oath, then, is *an end of all strife* or 'gainsaying', for it reveals the serious intention and determination of the person behind the oath.

17. This method of oath-taking in human affairs, which is so decisive in bringing to an end all strife, is adopted by God to prove to believers, or to *the heirs of promise*, the unchangeable nature of His sovereign decree more convincingly than He could have done by the simple giving of the promise. Calvin limits this oath to the Jews, but the expression 'we might have' in the following verse is against this. Both promise and oath are spiritual, and are for the benefit of all Abraham's faithful sons, his spiritual seed belonging to all ages. Both the RV and RSV state that God 'interposed with an oath', i.e. between the divine purpose and promise and human weakness God placed His oath as a guarantee that His purpose would be accomplished and His promise fulfilled.

18–20. God's promise and oath are the *two immutable things*, the two unchangeable spiritual realities, the two unalterable facts *in which it was impossible for God to lie* (or deceive). The unchangeable God is faithful, His word is sure and always dependable, but when it is confirmed by an oath it is even more worthy of our trust. In all this the weakest Christian should find *strong consolation* and comfort.

Two metaphors are now used to give further encouragement. The first, which is usually associated with Numbers xxxv, refers to certain offenders fleeing to the cities of refuge. For *who have fled* Knox has 'wanderers', but the persons concerned are in fact fleeing from some fearful judgment or dreadful calamity, like the guilty sinner fleeing from the judgment of his sins to the safe and sure refuge of Jesus Christ. It suits the context better, therefore, if the metaphor is that of mariners fleeing from storm and tempest to some covert or harbour (cf. Is. iv. 6). The second metaphor is that of an *anchor* of a ship which, when dropped into the sea, lays hold of the bottom and brings security to the ship and those on board.

Hope is the Christian's *sure and stedfast* anchor which has found a firm hold in the forerunner who has entered within the veil for us. The high priest, acting according to God's command, entered within the veil as man's representative. Christ did all this and more, for He was our forerunner, a link and a pledge. He is the Christian's link between the visible and invisible, and a certain pledge that one day the believer will also enter within the veil to share His eternal glory.

VI. CHRIST'S PRIESTHOOD, MINISTRY AND SACRIFICE (vii. 1–x. 18)

Christ's superiority over the three great aspects of the ritual system—priesthood, ministry and sacrifice—is now discussed. His priesthood is greater than the Aaronic, for it is after the order of Melchisedec according to a divine oath which has never been revoked (vii). His ministry is superior, for it is spiritual and eternal, not earthly and temporary (viii–ix). His sacrifice is also superior, for it was one sacrifice, not many, offered once for all time, not often (x. 1–18).

a. The superiority of Christ's priesthood (vii. 1–28)

The characteristics of Melchisedec and his superiority over Abraham are presented in verses 1–3. This is followed by a discussion on the fourfold superiority of the Melchisedec priesthood over the Aaronic (4–10). The author then passes from a consideration of Melchisedec's priesthood to that of Christ; he shows how His priesthood is greater and also how it supersedes the Aaronic (11–28).

i. The characteristics of the priesthood of Melchisedec

(**vii. 1–3**). The Jews attached high honour to *this Melchisedec*. Philo spoke of him as a type of the Logos or Word, yet his name appears only twice in the Old Testament. It is mentioned in Genesis xiv. 18–20 in connection with Abraham's intervention on behalf of the inhabitants of the district in which Lot, Abraham's nephew, lived. It is found again in Psalm cx. 4, which shows that in the Psalmist's day the order of the Melchisedec priesthood was known. Two important titles of Melchisedec are briefly mentioned—*king of Salem* and *priest of the most high God*. This dual capacity of Melchisedec was not possible under the Jewish religion, for in it kingship was separate from priesthood.[1] This dual office appears in Psalm cx which, as it was in the mind of the writer, implies that he thought of Christ as the King-Priest. The title *the most high God*, which appears in Genesis xiv. 18, also appears in Genesis xiv. 22 where Jehovah is spoken of as *the most high God*, i.e. 'God the supreme', and not 'the highest of the gods'. This title of Jehovah was also used by the Phoenicians, and it is evident that the worship of the one true God was not confined to the family of Abraham.

In his office of priesthood Melchisedec blesses, as one having the right to bless, just as Aaron as high priest and all the priests had a right 'to bless (the people) in the name of the Lord' (Dt. xxi. 5). In addition Melchisedec, a Gentile, was recognized as a true priest of Jehovah by Abraham and given a tithe of all the spoil. The writer views such an action by the father of the Jewish race as an acknowledgment of Melchisedec's superiority. The two titles *King of righteousness* and *King of Salem* make Melchisedec a fit type of the Messiah who is called 'The Lord our righteousness' (Je. xxiii. 6, xxxiii. 16); and the immediate result of this righteousness in His kingdom is peace (Is. ix. 5, 6, xxxii. 17).

3. The writer, accepting the Alexandrian principle that the very silence of Scripture is charged with meaning, takes advantage of the absence in Genesis of any reference to Melchisedec's parents, birth and death to suggest the independence

[1] There are indications, however, that for a time the union was restored under the Maccabeans, yet neither royalty nor priesthood at that time came through proper channels.

and the timelessness of his priesthood. The fathers and mothers of the Levitical priesthood could easily be traced, for their genealogy was carefully preserved. We learn from Ezra ii. 62, 63; Nehemiah vii. 63–65 that those who could not clearly prove their proper line of descent were not allowed to officiate till the matter was settled. Melchisedec belongs to no priestly family, his priesthood does not depend upon succession, nor is it subject to mortality, *having neither beginning of days, nor end of life*. The time that the sons of Levi commenced their ministration could always be traced; so could the conclusion of these ministrations for, if they did not end at an appointed time, they certainly ended at death. Melchisedec, as there is no record of his death, *abideth a priest continually*. The suggestion that invests Melchisedec with a typical resemblance of Jesus Christ, who as God has no mother and as man has no father, should be rejected as contrary to the whole purpose of the writer. It is in the timelessness of the priesthood that Melchisedec resembles the Son of God.

ii. The superiority of the Melchisedec priesthood (vii. 4–10). A fourfold superiority of the Melchisedec priesthood is now presented. Firstly, Abraham gave him tithes, thus acknowledging his priestly office, and in this respect his religious superiority. Secondly, Melchisedec blessed him, and the less is blessed by the greater because as a priest of God he was divinely commissioned to communicate such blessings. Thirdly, under the law, the Aaronic priesthood was temporary; but before the law was instituted Melchisedec's priesthood was perpetual. Lastly, in Abraham, Levi, who received tithes from the sons of Abraham, paid tithes to Melchisedec.

4. The oratorical imperative *consider* suggests that we should contemplate spiritually those things which are visibly portrayed in the ancient narrative, especially the greatness of Melchisedec. This greatness stands clearly revealed when even Abraham—the great patriarch, the friend of God, the founder

of the Jewish nation, and the father of all them that believe—
paid the best part of the spoils to him.

5. The Levites were the lineal descendants of Abraham and
from among them came those who received the sacred dignity
of the priest's office, i.e. those who were of the household of
Aaron. In this office they have a charge *according to* (or in) *the
law* to tithe the people. Melchisedec possessed greater honour,
for the dignity of his office was acknowledged by Abraham.
It may be true that, after the Exile, the priests themselves col-
lected the *tithes*, for Jewish tradition says that they did so from
the time of Ezra; but this does not necessarily contradict the
statement here. The usual procedure was for the Levites *to
take tithes* and the priests took a tithe of that tithe. If the priests
took tithes from the people through the Levites they were in
actual fact taking tithes from the people. There is no need,
therefore, to alter *people* (*laon*) into Levi (*Leuin*) as some have
done to overcome the supposed difficulty.

6, 7. Here and in verse 9 the writer makes use of Greek
perfects to suggest that what is written is still speaking and,
therefore, is still relevant. Past events in Scripture can have a
living message for any age, 'for whatsoever things were written
aforetime were written for our learning' (Rom. xv. 4). The
promise that in Abraham's seed all the families of the earth
were to be blessed (Gn. xii. 3) and a further promise that his
seed would possess the land for ever (Gn. xiii. 14 ff.) reveal
vividly Abraham's greatness. Yet even so he is blessed by
Melchisedec, and as *the less is blessed of the better* so Melchisedec
in his office as priest is superior to Abraham.

8. Reference is now made to the mortality of the Aaronic
priests and the immortality of Melchisedec. *Here* refers to the
Levitical system which was in use at the time of writing, thus
suggesting that the Epistle was probably written before AD 70.
There refers to the time of the Melchisedec priesthood which

preceded the institution of the Aaronic priesthood. The fact that no descent of Melchisedec is given, no date of birth, no mention of death at a time when these were considered of supreme importance can be ascribed only to the work of the Holy Spirit whose object was figuratively to show beforehand that the priesthood to which Christ belonged was before, superior to, and continues after the Levitical.

9, 10. The expression *And as I may so say* (RSV, 'One might even say') implies that the following statement about Levi must not be taken literally but allegorically; and even when taken in the latter sense it must not be pressed too far. 'It apologises while it speaks' (Vaughan). When Abraham paid tithes to Melchisedec, Levi was not born; yet by his own special, and somewhat unusual, manner of reckoning the writer maintains that, as he was in Abraham's loins, he also paid tithes to Melchisedec, and therefore Melchisedec's priesthood is superior to the Levitical. We must not think of Levi here as an individual only, but as the representative and ancestor of the Jewish priesthood. Two things stand out for consideration: first, the Scriptures sometimes possess a meaning which can be found only below the surface of the literal meaning. Second, this passage is strongly in favour of the viewpoint that this Epistle was written for Jewish readers.

iii. A comparison between the legal and spiritual priesthoods (vii. 11–28). The writer now takes a bold step by asserting that the Levitical priesthood was to be superseded. This meant disannulling not only the Levitical priesthood but also the whole Mosaic system of law, which was received on the basis of this priesthood (11–14). Thus a spiritual and royal priesthood was to take the place of the legal and sacerdotal (15–17). The superiority of the former over the latter is brought out in a threefold manner: it introduced a better hope by means of which we can draw near to God (18, 19); it rested upon a divine oath, and no such oath is mentioned in connection with the Levitical priesthood (20–22); Christ's Priesthood is unchangeable, for He ever liveth (23–25).

11, 12. The Melchisedec priesthood appeared in history in Genesis xiv, but with the advent of the Levitical it disappears completely from the Scriptural record except for one brief quotation in Psalm cx. 4. Yet this former kind of priesthood, being superior to and not so limited as the Jewish, was destined to play the greater part in church history, though not in the type Melchisedec but in the antitype Jesus Christ. *Perfection* is a necessary characteristic of the true and final priesthood, which when it has come has no successor. The Levitical cannot be this priesthood for *another* that is 'a different one' has arisen. Perfection was not one of its characteristics for it failed to establish an eternal covenant and to provide a permanent access into God's presence. *Under* or 'on the basis of' the Levitical priesthood *the people received the law*, which means the whole law of Moses of which the Levitical priesthood with its ritual was the centre. It is, in fact, more; it is the pillar upon which the Mosaic system rests. The Levitical priesthood has been superseded, and with its fall is included the whole constitution, not merely the ceremonial.

13. To support the revolutionary statement that the Levitical priesthood and the Mosaic law had in God's sight lost their validity it is stated that Christ, whose priesthood was different, *pertaineth* (RSV 'belonged') *to another tribe*. Both prophecy and the Gospels bear witness to this fact and show that the other tribe is none other than the royal tribe of Judah (cf. Is. ix. 6, 7, xi. 1–5; Mi. v. 2; Mt. ii. 5–6; Rom. i. 3 etc.). Few will deny the underlying truth of Westcott's suggestion, which has the support of ii. 14, that *meteschēken*, *pertaineth*, points to the voluntary assumption of humanity, and of the tribe of Judah, by our Lord. Whether by his use of *meteschēken* the writer thought of this is doubtful, though the use of the perfect certainly suggests that our Lord has permanently a share in that tribe.

No-one of this tribe ever at any time performed priestly functions. Such functions were confined to those who belonged to
the tribe of Levi. As Christ did not belong to this tribe His
ministry could never take place at Jewish altars.

14. Owen and others maintain that *prodēlon*, *evident*, means
'manifest beforehand', thus giving a temporal meaning to *pro*.
It has been shown above that our Lord's descent *out of Juda*
was made known beforehand, and familiarity with well-
known prophecies would help to underline this fact concerning Christ's descent; yet the use of the perfect in this verse
shows that it was an accomplished and acknowledged fact and
not an inference from prophecy. It is not necessary, therefore,
to give a temporal sense to *pro* in *prodēlon*. It appears that
anatetalken, *sprang*, or 'hath sprung', when applied to Christ's
appearance in the New Testament, is always connected with
light. It has, therefore, been suggested that *anatetalken* must
bear a similar meaning here and that Christ came out of the
tribe of Judah like the rising of the sun or a star. Yet it may
refer to the prophetic figure of the Branch which, like a grow-
ing plant, springs out of the roots of Jesse (Is. xi. 1; Zc. iii. 8,
vi. 12; Je. xxiii. 5, 6).

15. Although the writer states that something is *far more
evident*, or 'more abundantly evident', it is not so clear what
that something really is. It can hardly be limited to the
difference between the Levitical priesthood and Christ's, as
Chrysostom suggests, nor can it simply mean that, while the
former priesthood is imperfect, Christ's is perfect. It most
probably means that the temporary character of the Levitical
priesthood, and the change of the whole Mosaic law, is more
abundantly evident from Psalm cx which speaks of *another* or
different priesthood which has no connection with the old law.

16. *The law of a carnal commandment* was the rule of the law or
constraining principle dealing with the Levitical priesthood

and, therefore, does not refer to the whole Mosaic law. For *carnal commandment* the RSV has 'bodily descent', but 'outward observance' is better, for the stress is upon the external or earthly features which include bodily descent, the continual removal by death and renewal of the Levitical priests, and also those earthly ceremonies which were to pass away. The contrast is then between the external aspect of the Levitical priesthood and the internal aspect of Christ's. Christ's priesthood does not rest upon the law of a dead letter—it is dynamic and rests upon God's oath. It does not depend upon bodily descent, which would have made it subject to change and death, but is indissoluble. It is true that our great High Priest offered Himself on the cross for man's sin according to God's purpose; but death could not hold Him, nor bring to an end His priesthood.

17. *For he testifieth* can refer only to God as the One who testifies; but as the verb is present passive indicative it is more correct to translate 'it is witnessed' and add 'of him' as does the RSV. Some have objected to this impersonal approach, and translate 'He is testified of', which has support from other parts of the Epistle. Knox has 'God says of Him' which, though difficult to derive from the Greek, gives the right meaning. For though 'it is witnessed' of Christ in the words of the prophecy found in Psalm cx, God was behind the prophecy.

A threefold superiority of Christ's priesthood is now shown. Firstly, it fulfils the purpose of priesthood by bringing men into God's presence. Secondly, its permanency is secure, for it is built upon God's oath which cannot be revoked. Thirdly, it is unchangeable. Thus the priesthood of Christ is perfect, eternal and unchangeable.

18, 19. By the proclamation of God that Christ was a priest after the order of Melchisedec *there is verily a disannulling of the commandment going before* (RSV, 'a former commandment is set aside'). According to Deissmann's examination of the papyri *athetēsis, disannulling,* is used in a technical, puristic sense which gives support to the AV. In ix. 26, the only other place in the New Testament where this word occurs, both the AV and RSV have 'to put away'. The same word should be used in both places. God's establishment of a priesthood after the order of Melchisedec meant that the commandment referring to the Levitical priesthood had been made void; it no longer had God's authority, and was deprived of any legal force. In the same way, in ix. 26, Christ by the sacrifice of Himself has made void sin; He has destroyed its power, and has made it as though it had never existed. The reason given for the rejection of the commandment was its *weakness and unprofitableness.* The weakness of the law is clearly illustrated by St. Paul in Romans vii, viii. 3 and Galatians iii. 23, 24. Its unprofitableness or uselessness is made plain by its inability to cleanse the conscience from sin, and to impart spiritual power that men may obey the law; but above all it failed to draw men near to God.

Yet there was a purpose in the 'former commandment', for it was a constituent part of the old covenant which preceded and led to the new covenant. It reminded the people of their sins even though it could not remove them; of their need of forgiveness, though it was deficient in providing the means; and of God's presence, though it failed to bring the people within the veil. It pointed the way to the *better hope* but was unable to provide it. This *better hope* arises from God's declaration that a different priesthood, which will enable men to *draw nigh unto God,* has been established. The great High Priest, who through the sacrifice of Himself dealt with the sin problem, is able, through His ascension, to bring all believers within the veil into God's holy presence. This is the first introduction to the theme of the priesthood of all believers, which is dealt with more fully in chapter x.

20, 21. The superior solemnity of the institution of Christ's priesthood indicates the superiority of that priesthood. It was based upon a divine oath which cannot be altered, for God

123

will not repent, i.e. change His mind. Such *an oath* as that sworn by God, is as eternal as the eternal God and indicates that the priesthood is eternal and thus more excellent than, and far superior to, the Levitical priesthood which did not rest upon any such oath and, therefore, could only be temporary. Both the RV and RSV correctly omit *after the order of Melchisedec* which follows *Thou art a priest for ever*, since it is an addition from verse 17.

22. *Jesus*, our great High Priest, *was made*, or 'has become' *a surety of a better testament* which has taken the place of the old. The Greek word *egguos, surety*, or 'guarantor', which does not occur elsewhere in the New Testament, has often been regarded as a synonym for 'mediator', but there is a difference between these words. A mediator is one who seeks to reconcile two parties at variance. He may place in the hand of each opposing party a security that the agreed terms of reconciliation will be honoured. John Owen alleged that Christ became surety to God for men when He vicariously took upon Himself the guilt of their sins. Others have declared that He became surety to man for God when He triumphantly rose from the dead and ascended to the right hand of God. All that is stated in our text is that Jesus Himself is a surety that a better covenant has been established by God. The greatness of His Person, the sufficiency of His sacrifice, the authority behind His resurrection, the superiority of His priesthood and His ascension to the throne of God are a complete pledge of the validity of the better covenant.

23, 24. The last point of the superiority of Christ's priesthood is now set before us. Under the old covenant the priests were many in number; under the new there is one. They were removed by death; but He abides, i.e. He lives for ever. Their priesthood passed to another; but His priesthood is *aparabatos, unchangeable*. This rare word is not found elsewhere in the Greek Bible. Many have translated it 'without a successor', 'not transferable'; but such a meaning is not found anywhere else. MM points out that the technical use compared with the later literary meaning constitutes a very strong case against the rendering 'not transferable'.

25, 26. *Wherefore*, i.e., because His priesthood is eternal, *he is able also to save them to the uttermost.* The phrase *eis to panteles*, *to the uttermost*, normally means 'completely', 'absolutely'; but it may have a temporal meaning as the RSV 'for all time' suggests, and this has the support of some ancient versions. Westcott's criticism that the old commentators strangely explain *eis to panteles* as if it were *eis to dienekes*, 'for ever', is not justifiable, for MM tell of a man who sells some property *apo tou nun eis to panteles*, 'from henceforth even for ever', and maintain that 'this would support a temporal meaning in Hebrews "to save finally", which suits well the *pantote* which follows'. Different views have also been expressed concerning the word with which *eis to panteles* should be connected. Most commentators combined it with *save*, translating as the AV or RSV. There are others, however, who link it with *able*, translating 'He is completely, or for ever, able to save'. There seems little, if any, difference in the meaning. Christ is able to save completely in time and for eternity.

Our great High Priest through His perfect sacrifice saves from the penalty of sin by the bestowal of forgiveness, and through the permanency of His life saves from the power of sin by the communication of grace and strength to those who have faith in Him and *come unto God by him*. This last phrase recalls Matthew xi. 28 'Come unto me' and John xiv. 6 'No man cometh unto the Father, but by me'. A further reason why our Lord is able to save is given in the words *seeing he ever liveth to make intercession*. This intercession is not the offering of Himself in the heavenly sanctuary (cf. viii. 2). The offering of Himself took place on the cross once and for all and can never be repeated (ix. 25–28, x. 10, 12, 14). According to Westcott some of the early fathers call attention to the contrasts which this verse includes between Christ's human and divine natures; and how His very presence before God in His humanity is in itself a prevailing intercession. This may be true, but the intercession in this verse is a direct representation to God by our great High Priest on behalf of those who have come to God through Him.

The High Priest whose characteristics have just been described is most suited to our needs. By His death in which He made purification for sins He can draw men near to God; by His experience of temptations and trials He can sympathize with His children in their infirmities; by His enthronement on high He can meet every need; by the permanency of His life He can save completely; and by His prevailing advocacy He can bring the blessings and favours of God upon all believers. The same High Priest is *holy*, for in all His actions for man on earth He displayed that moral character which honoured God's holiness. He is *harmless*, for in all His actions towards man He showed before them a life perfectly innocent, free from all craft and malice. He is *undefiled*, for in His official position as High Priest He was not stained by any kind of impurity, having no defilement in Himself. Moffatt suggests that the language may be intended to suggest a contrast between the deep ethical purity of Jesus and the ritual purity of the Levitical high priest, who had to take extreme precautions against outward defilement.

Thus in His life, character and office He is *separate from sinners*. This last phrase could mean that Christ by His exaltation has been removed from all contact with sinful men so that He cannot be defiled by them, and ix. 28 may support this. Certainly the use of the perfect suggests that He is permanently separated from them; but Christ's exaltation hardly implies this. Moreover, in the light of Christ's sinlessness upon earth, it seems strange that He should be exalted to heaven to avoid defilement. Christ by His perfect piety towards God, by His perfect justice and benevolence towards men, and by the perfection and completeness of His great sacrifice, is in a class separate from sinners. Our great High Priest with such perfect qualifications is worthy of the highest honour, authority and power. By being *made higher than the heavens* this position is now His.

27. It seems that the writer by his use of *to offer up sacrifice, first for his own sins, and then for the people's* had in mind the day of atonement which took place annually, when the high priest offered sacrifice for himself and for his fellow Israelites (ix. 7, 25, x. 1, 3). The insertion of *kath hēmeran, daily*, shows, however, that the statement cannot be confined to this annual event. To suggest that it means 'on a definite day each year' is scarcely a way out of the difficulty, for if the writer had meant this why did he use *kath hēmeran* and not *kat'eniauton*, 'year by year' as he does in ix. 25? The verse says quite clearly that Christ need not do daily what the Levitical high priests do daily. The writer has simply blended together the yearly sacrifice of the high priest and the daily sacrifices of the priests. These subordinate priests were merely substitutes for the high priest who was head of all. It does appear from Exodus xxix. 38, 44; Leviticus vi. 19–22; and Josephus, *History of the Jewish War*, v. 5, 7 that the high priest might take actual part in the daily offerings. Indeed, Leviticus vi. 19–22 LXX states that the high priest was to 'offer to the Lord . . . the tenth part of an ephah of fine flour for a sacrifice continually, the half of it in the morning and the half of it in the evening . . .' But there is no necessity for our Lord to offer sacrifices daily for the sins of the people, *for this he did once, when he offered up himself*; neither was there any need for Him to offer *for his own sins*, for He had no sin. The Son of God became man to proclaim the new covenant. As High Priest of this covenant *he offered up himself* to establish it. Thus a new thought is introduced of Christ as Priest and Victim which is found neither in the Melchisedec nor in the Aaronic priesthoods.

28. The writer who commenced the chapter with the king-priest closes it with the divine priest uniting the two prophecies of Psalms ii and cx together. A contrast is then made between the one Son of God, our great High Priest, and the many high priests, between His perfectness and their weakness, between His divinity and their humanity. The AV seems to have derived *consecrated for evermore* from the use of the verb *teleioō* in Exodus xxix. 22; Leviticus viii. 22, xvi. 10 LXX, where it has the same meaning as the Hebrew expression 'to fill the hands', i.e. 'to consecrate'. Yet 'perfected for evermore' (RV) seems preferable, for *teleioō* has that meaning in ii. 10. Moulton rightly says, 'We are not to understand that Jesus was first "perfected" and then appointed as High Priest: this would contradict what has just been taught (verse 27), for it was as High Priest that He offered the sacrifice of Himself.'

b. The ministry of Christ (viii. 1–ix. 28)

It has been shown that Christ has the true qualifications of priesthood and that His priesthood is superior to the Levitical because He Himself is superior to the Levitical priests. The writer now discusses the ministry of the great High Priest and the place in which this ministry is performed. He finds a proof that Christ's ministry is superior because He ministers in a superior place (viii. 1–6). Further aspects of superiority are seen in the threefold pre-eminence of the new covenant over the old (viii. 7–13). A more detailed description is then given of the earthly and heavenly tabernacles (ix. 1–10) and of the better ministry (ix. 11–28).

i. The great High Priest in the true Holy of holies (viii. 1–6).

Christ's act in taking the throne was for the writer the consummation of the sacrificial aspect of His high priestly work (1). His earthly ministry having come to an end, His heavenly ministry commences in the sanctuary into which He has entered having offered Himself as a sacrifice for sin (2, 3). His ministry no longer being sacrificial could not take place in the earthly tabernacle, which was confined to the priests of the law. It is enacted in the real and true sanctuary (4, 5). This ministry is 'better', for the covenant of which He is the mediator is better and rests upon 'better' promises (6).

1. *Kephalaion, this is the sum,* can either mean a summary, i.e. of the points of an argument, or the chief point in a discussion. As the writer proceeds to discuss a new point in his discourse, and little or no recapitulation takes place, 'chief point' is preferable to *the sum.* The inclusion of the article by the RV, which translates 'the chief point', is quite permissible but could be misleading if taken to mean that the action of Christ in taking the throne was superior to His priesthood and sacrifice on the cross. No thought of the superiority of one aspect of Christ's work over another was in the writer's mind. He is simply stating that Christ has consummated His great sacrificial work on the cross by taking the seat *on the right hand of the throne of the Majesty in the heavens.* In i. 3 where the Son's honour and glory are in mind, no mention is made of *throne.* In xii. 2 where the kingly power of Jesus is brought out, *Majesty* is omitted. The inclusion of both *throne* and *Majesty* indicates that the kingly power and dominion of the great High Priest of the Christian Church has crowned the office of priesthood with supreme excellence and dignity.

2. Though Christ sits on the throne He is nevertheless *a minister of the sanctuary, and of the true tabernacle. Leitourgos, minister,* does not necessarily mean a sacrificial ministry, although in the LXX, where it is used of the ministrations of the priests and Levites, sacrificial functions must be included. In classical Greek *leitourgos* was used of various forms of public service, and such uses are found in the New Testament (cf. Lk. i. 23; Rom. xiii. 6; 2 Cor. ix. 12). Its use of Christ's ministry in the sanctuary does not mean a sacerdotal ministry, nor does it mean that our Lord is at the heavenly altar presenting His eternal offering as Manson suggests. The sacrificial aspect of our Lord's ministry was performed and completed when He offered Himself once and for all on the cross. The ministry which our great High Priest now performs is one of intercession and of presenting the prayers of His children before His Father. Westcott rightly says, 'Before His session our Lord fulfilled the Levitical priesthood by the offering of Himself. After His session He fulfilled the royal priesthood of Melchisedec.'

Some commentators have taken *tōn hagiōn, the sanctuary,* to be masculine and translate 'the saints'. The word is most certainly neuter, yet it does not mean 'holy things', as Luther suggests, but the heavenly antitype of the earthly Holy of holies. *True*, having the same meaning as in John i. 9, is not in opposition to what is false but is the antithesis to what is earthly and secondary. It is the archetype which exists in heaven in contrast to the earthly image of the holy place (see Additional Note, p. 133).

3. The purpose for which every high priest is ordained ('is appointed', RSV) is to offer on man's behalf (cf. v. 1). Our Lord has been appointed High Priest by God, therefore it was necessary that He should offer on behalf of man. This He did once and for all by the sacrifice of Himself. The AV, RV and RSV supply *estin, it is,* with *anangkaion,* 'necessary'. The Peshito correctly inserts *ēn, was,* which is more in harmony with the aorist *prosenegkai* which immediately follows. The author is most careful in his use of tenses; therefore, when he uses the aorist, it suggests a single finished act of offering. Westcott favours this when he says, 'If the reference is to the Cross, as seems to be required by the type and context, then *ēn* must be supplied.' If there had been any intention on the part of the writer to show that our great High Priest's offering was to be made continuously or repeatedly, he would have used not the aorist but the present as he does in ix. 25 where he speaks of a continual offering. The position of Christ sitting at the right hand of God speaks of one who has finished the sacrificial aspect of His ministry. This is very different from the Levitical priests who always remained standing (cf. x. 11, 12). Strangely enough Manson in speaking of our forerunner on the other side of the veil says, 'He atones and intercedes for us'. Yet this conception of Christ atoning in 'the true tabernacle' has no foundation in this Epistle nor in any other part of the New Testament. Calvin's approach is certainly better. 'He suffered', he says, 'death as men do, but as a priest He atoned for the sins of the world in a divine manner; there was an external shedding of blood, but there was also an internal and spiritual purgation; in a word He died on earth, but the virtue and efficacy of His death proceeded from heaven.'

4. The priesthood of Christ, which is after the order of Melchisedec, cannot be limited to an earthly priesthood; indeed, *if* Christ *were on earth, he should not be a priest,* i.e. after the Levitical order. The earthly place of ministration appointed by God was the Jewish tabernacle and, according to the law, the ministrations within this sacred edifice were performed only by those who were of the seed of Aaron, of the tribe of Levi. As Christ was not of this tribe He could not minister in the earthly tabernacle (cf. vii. 13, 14). Calvin takes the view that the writer meant either that Christ was not a priest, while the priesthood continued, as He had no sacrifice, or that the sacrifices of the law ceased as soon as Christ appeared. He finds the first proposition untenable and maintains 'the Levitical order is now abolished'.

5. As Christ's present ministry cannot take place in the earthly tabernacle it must be performed in heaven. This is no loss but real gain, for the earthly tabernacle at its best is merely a 'copy' or 'model' of the true *tabernacle* in which Christ now ministers. This earthly tabernacle was not false, but incomplete, and represented imperfectly its heavenly counterpart. It was just a *shadow* of the reality or, as Moffatt says, 'a shadowy outline', a secondhand inferior reproduction.
  Chrēmatizein, admonished ('instructed', RSV), is used both in

the LXX and New Testament of divine communications, instructions and warnings (cf. Je. xxxii. 30 (LXX), xxxvii. 2; Mt. ii. 22; Lk. ii. 26; Acts x. 22; Heb. xii. 25). Now these three aspects of the word appear in the supernatural revelation given to Moses about the tabernacle. He received a divine communication which contained instructions as to how the tabernacle should be made, yet it contained a warning that *all things* should be made *according to the pattern* which was revealed *in the mount*. Calvin maintains that 'See . . . that thou make all things according to the pattern' carries with it the further meaning 'see that thou do nothing beyond the pattern'.

Much speculation has arisen over the heavenly *pattern* which was shown to Moses in the Mount (cf. Ex. xxv. 40, xxvi. 30; Nu. viii. 4). Was it a copy of 'the true tabernacle' or was it a copy of a copy? The Scriptures are silent on this point and dogmatism must be ruled out; but the materialistic view of the Palestinian Jews, who maintained that there was in heaven a literal counterpart of the earthly tabernacle, should be rejected. Philo and the Alexandrian Jews seem to have made use of this verse and of Plato's doctrine of ideas in an endeavour to combine Judaism with Platonic conception; but although there may be an Alexandrian element in it, yet there seems nothing in the context which could not be found in the Old Testament and Jewish apocalyptic thought.

6. The superiority of Christ's *ministry* has been shown by the 'reality' of the place in which He ministers and by the removal of earthly limitations. Another aspect is now introduced to show that in proportion as the new covenant is better than the old, so much the more is Christ's ministry *more excellent* than the Levitical. The new covenant is better, for it has been established through the *mediator* Christ Jesus, whereas the Sinai covenant was established through the mediator Moses (cf. Gal. iii. 19, 20). Christ's superiority over Moses has already been discussed (cf. iii. 1–6). Further important factors are now considered. The Mosaic *covenant* was a covenant of law, but the new is a covenant of promise and the Son of God is the surety that the promises will be fulfilled. The old covenant though educative was impotent and temporary, the new covenant is redemptive, dynamic and eternal.

Already in this Epistle Christ has been portrayed as Mediator of creation, revelation and redemption (i. 1–3). Westcott says, 'The limited office of "the Mediator of a covenant" suggests the thought of the wider work of a Mediator "of the relation of God to creation".' It is usual in the New Testament to regard Christ as the agent of creation; but in ii. 10 and Romans xi. 36 God is seen as the origin, the agent and the object of all things. In Galatians i. 1; Colossians i. 16 there is an interchange of attributes. Philo through his emphasis on God as pure spirit, and through the influence of Plato's dualism, divorced God and matter; and therefore without mediation of some kind God could not act upon matter. But this is a departure from the biblical view. Westcott stated that Philo's theory of the Word standing between the creature and the Father of all, the messenger of divine order and the inspirer of human life, is the finest view of the relation of the world to its Maker apart from the incarnation. Yet for Philo the 'Word' or 'divine logos' was nothing more than a philosophical abstraction and very different from the personal Mediator of the new covenant.

Additional note: 'The true tabernacle' (viii. 2)

The true tabernacle, which the Lord pitched, and not man has had many interpretations. It has been suggested that it signifies the Church, either militant or triumphant. 1 Corinthians iii. 17, xii. 27; Ephesians iv. 4, v. 30 speak of the Church as the body of Christ and as the temple of the Holy Spirit; but there is little scriptural evidence to suggest that it is the true tabernacle. The Holy Spirit certainly ministers through His Church on earth, but there is no suggestion that this is the antitype of the earthly tabernacle. The same can be said of the Church triumphant in heaven. Furthermore, there is no evidence that the ministry of the Holy Spirit in the Church militant continues in the Church triumphant.

Luther, influenced by 1 Thessalonians v. 23, made the tripartite nature of the Christian the antitype of the earthly tabernacle. The Christian's spirit, he maintained, is *sanctum sanctorum* (the Holy of holies), God's dwelling-place. His soul is *sanctum* (the holy place) in which are seven lights such as reason, understanding, etc. His body is *atrium* (the outer court) which is open and patent to all. It is difficult to see how the true tabernacle fits into Luther's division or how it can in reality be connected with the earthly tabernacle. In 2 Corinthians v. 1 and 4 it is the body which is likened to a tabernacle not the whole man.

Some commentators have identified the true tabernacle with the 'greater and more perfect tabernacle' mentioned in ix. 11, but it is better to take *dia*, 'through', in that verse in a local sense and refer it to the visible heavens through which Christ passed into the Holy of Holies, into the presence of God Himself. This is supported by 'Since then we have a great high priest who has passed through the heavens, Jesus . . .' (iv. 14, RSV). The difficulty in this is the fact that 'the visible heavens' are a part of 'this creation'. It is possible that the author conceived 'the visible heavens' as not belonging to the earthly created world and that he used *ktisis* in the sense of 'building'. As the high priest passed through the tabernacle so Christ passed through a greater and more perfect tabernacle—the visible heavens.

Others who identify the true tabernacle with the 'greater and more perfect tabernacle' intimate that the humanity of Christ is meant. There is much to be said for this point of view, for in John ii. 21 Christ speaks of the 'temple of his body'. In Mark xiv. 58 *acheiropoiēton*, 'made without hands' is the same word as is used in ix. 11, though the use of the negative is different. 2 Corinthians v. 1, 4 likens the human body to a tabernacle, and John i. 14 mentions that 'the Word was made flesh, and dwelt (tabernacled) among us.' 'The veil' through which we have a new and living way into the most holy place is said to be Christ's 'flesh' (x. 19, 20).

It is possible to identify *the true tabernacle* with the humanity of Christ without identifying this with the 'greater and more perfect tabernacle'. The human body of Christ was, however, certainly of this creation. The argument put forward by Oecumenius that under different aspects the Lord's body was, and was not, 'of this creation' may partly overcome this difficulty, but it raises far more serious problems. Such an interpretation gives an unnatural meaning to 'body' which affects the true humanity of Christ and is a form of docetism. Even if this is connected with the glorified body of Christ the same problem arises, and if His body is different from the body which came forth from the grave, then the problem of the resurrection arises.

In the Old Testament 'the Holy of holies' signifies God's presence, but when *skēnē, tabernacle*, is joined with 'meeting' it implies the place of revelation, or when it is joined with 'witness' it implies the revelation itself. It is highly probable that *the sanctuary* and *the true tabernacle* (viii. 2) do not refer to the same thing. 'The sanctuary' is the antitype of the earthly Holy of holies and, therefore, suggests God's presence. Our great High Priest has passed through the great and more perfect tabernacle, the visible heavens, into this sanctuary. *The true tabernacle* signifies the humanity of Christ in whom and through whom the full and unceasing revelation of God takes place.

ii. The two covenants (viii. 7–13). The weakness of the Israelites and the imperfection of the old covenant are the reasons given for the inauguration of the better covenant which is established upon better promises. By the promise of forgiveness of sins man's deepest spiritual need is met (12). By the promise of an inward power man's weakness is overcome (10). By the promise of possession security is assured (10). By the promise of a fuller and deeper revelation direct fellowship with God is guaranteed (11).

7, 8. The inauguration of the new covenant was proof that the *first covenant* was not *faultless*. The prophets had recognized its limitations and ineffectiveness (see Je. xxxi. 31–34). It could reveal sin but not remove it, and being defective it could not save or justify guilty sinners. It failed to meet the deepest needs of sinful man. In Romans vii the law is described as holy, just, good and spiritual, but sin had made it ineffective. The real cause of the covenant's weakness was man's sinfulness; therefore God finds *fault with them*, i.e. with the Israelites who failed to keep the covenant. Some have suggested that God finds fault with the covenant and tells the people so. This is possible grammatically, but it probably arose from a desire to bring verse 8 into harmony with verse 7. Because of the continued failure of the Israelites to keep the covenant and the ineffectiveness of the law to enable them to keep the covenant, *he saith* (i.e. God, not Jeremiah) *I will make a new covenant*.

9. Under the new covenant another exodus, different from the first, was initiated by God, and the reason given for such an action was the continual failure of the Israelites which compelled God to annul the first covenant—He *regarded them not*. This last quotation from Jeremiah follows the LXX, for the AV translation of Jeremiah xxxi. 32, following the Hebrew, has 'although I was an husband unto them'. Westcott supports the LXX on the ground that it fits in best with the context 'though', he concludes, 'the common reading can be explained'.

10–12. The threefold superiority of the new covenant over the old is now revealed in the threefold superiority of the promises. The first promise made the new covenant spiritual and inward, for God says, *I will put my laws into their mind, and write them in their hearts*. This dynamic was lacking in the old covenant, for though the law could reveal with vivid clearness the ways of good and evil, it failed to give to the Israelites the power which would have enabled them to do the good and resist the evil. On the contrary, as the forbidden fruit held real attractions for Eve, so the forbidden ways of the law held similar attractions. Romans vii shows that it is possible to delight in the law of God with the inward man yet at the same time submit to another law which makes war against the law of the mind. A new power was needed and is supplied under the new covenant. This power is not impersonal, but is in fact the third Person of the Trinity, the Holy Spirit, who enables the believer to resist the attractions and overcome the power of evil. It is the authority of the Spirit of life who through union with Christ Jesus makes us free from the power of sin which ends in death (Rom. viii. 2, 3). It is possible that the *mind* covers the intellect, and the *heart* the will and affections, for the new law of God was to be effective in the whole spiritual life of the Christian.

The Church under the new covenant is God's own possession, having been bought by the blood of Jesus (cf. Eph. i. 14; 1 Pet. i. 18 f.). The privilege of being God's people brings real security, for they are the special object of His love and protection. A similar idea of ownership is found in the Old Testament—God said of Israel, 'Then ye shall be a peculiar treasure unto me above all people' (Ex. xix. 5; cf. Ex. vi. 7). Hosea compares the relationship between God and His people to a marriage bond. Jeremiah sees the end of the marriage bond, which had been broken by Israel through her unfaithfulness, so that God ended the relationship. The Church, however, is in a more favourable position, for it possesses that inward dynamic which enables it to keep the covenant and remain faithful to God.

The new covenant removed the barrier between the holy God and sinful man. This was related to the sacrifice of Christ on the cross where He shed His blood. The acceptance of the terms of the new covenant brings a true experience of God. This experience of God is to continue, for by the second promise, *for all shall know me*, provision is made for all believers to receive a fuller and deeper revelation of unusual efficacy (see 1 Jn. ii. 27). The personal experience of God is no longer confined to a sacerdotal priesthood *for all shall know* the Lord, and the Holy Spirit, who teaches all things and whose anointing they have received, shall be their teacher.

By the use of *for* the suggestion is made that the promise of forgiveness is the foundation of all the other promises. The words *I will be merciful to their unrighteousness* show that the source of forgiveness is not human merit but God's mercy and grace. The ground of forgiveness is not man's repentance but the sacrifice of Christ. It is the new covenant which gives full and complete assurance that God will remember our *sins and . . . iniquities . . . no more.* The words *and their iniquities* are omitted by the best authorities and may have been added here from x. 17.

13. The pronouncement by God that He would make a new covenant implied that *he hath made the first old,* that is, antiquated, out of date, obsolete. The pronouncement took place in Jeremiah's day, and the working out took about six hundred years. Well might the author say that it was expiring of old age. Robertson says, 'The author writes as if the Old Testament legal and ceremonial system were about to vanish before the new covenant of grace. If he wrote after AD 70, would he not have written "has vanished away"?'

iii. The first tabernacle and its ministry (ix. 1–10). A detailed description of the component parts of the earthly tabernacle is given (1–5). The limitations of the priestly ministry within the two parts of the tabernacle are shown (6, 7). In all this there is a divine lesson that the old covenant was not perfect (8). The limitations of the priestly ministry apply also to the sacrifices which they offered (9, 10).

1. The use of *prōtē, first,* contrasts *the first covenant* with the new covenant, just as in verse 2 it contrasts 'the holy place' with 'the Holy of holies'. Some Greek MSS have 'tabernacle' for *covenant* (which is not in the Greek), but the similarity of thought with viii. 13 and beyond that with viii. 7 f. indicates that the context requires *covenant*.

The inclusion of *kai*, *also*, by the AV is doubtful, and is out of harmony with the writer's purpose which is to show that the ritual provisions of the old order have passed away completely. It is omitted by the Vaticanus MS, by the Chester Beatty papyrus and by the minuscule 1739, and this evidence is considerable in Hebrews. Moffatt, however, includes it, suggesting that *kai* before *hē prōtē*, the first, emphasizes the fact that the old had this in common with the new, viz. worship and a sanctuary, and that 'the writer takes a special view of the covenant which involves a celestial counterpart to the ritual provisions of the old order'. Zuntz's comment 'the inclusion of *kai* implies the very opposite of the writer's argument which was to show that the Jewish worship is superseded by the sacrifice of Christ' is much nearer the author's meaning than Moffatt's. He continues, 'There is no hint here, or anywhere else throughout the Epistle, that the worship of the synagogue is *continued* (not even on a higher plane) by the Christians.'

The first covenant had *ordinances of divine service* or 'regulations for worship' (RSV) which had the stamp of divine authority upon them, yet they, and the tabernacle in which they were performed, were *kosmikon*, *worldly*, a word which does not here imply enmity with God as it sometimes does elsewhere. It is used in the sense of belonging to the visible world, i.e. earthly, material, and thus indicating something imperfect and temporary.

2. The tabernacle itself was divided into the holy place and the Holy of holies. The AV calls the first part *the sanctuary*, but this is misleading, and it is better to place 'outer' before it to distinguish it from the inner sanctuary; but it clarifies the two parts if, as in RV, the first is called 'the Holy place' and the second 'the Holy of holies'. The outer part of the tabernacle contained *the candlestick, and the table, and the shewbread*. It also contained the altar of incense, which is not mentioned here (cf. verse 4). Both parts of the tabernacle were without windows, but only the first part needed *the candlestick* (or 'lampstand'), for the second part was illuminated by the glory of God. In Solomon's temple the number of candlesticks seems to have been ten (1 Ki. vii. 49; 2 Ch. iv. 7). Into this part the priests were allowed to enter; they were excluded only from the Holy of holies. *The table, and the shewbread* refers to the table upon which was set out the shewbread in two rows before God, and to the bread which was eaten in the holy place by the priests (cf. Ex. xxv. 23–30; Lv. xxiv. 5–9).

3. The second part of the tabernacle was *called the Holiest of all* and was *after the second veil*. *Meta, after,* used only here with a spatial reference, has the meaning of 'beyond' or 'behind'. Only the high priest was allowed to pass beyond this veil, and that privilege was confined to the day of atonement. The veil typified and represented the barrier between the holy God and sinful man, and revealed that the ritualism of the old covenant could not provide for the people a permanent way into God's presence. Matthew xxvii. 51 tells us that at Christ's death the veil of the temple was rent 'from the top to the bottom'.

4. The statement of the author that the Holy of holies *had the golden censer* has created a difficulty. Leviticus xvi. 12 mentions that the high priest on the day of atonement was to take a censer within the veil, but nowhere is this called *a golden censer*. In the inscriptions, papyri and classical Greek the meaning of *thumiatērion* seems to be *censer*. This meaning is also found in 2 Chronicles xxvi. 19; Exodus viii. 11 (LXX). Yet both Philo and Josephus give it the meaning of 'altar of incense'. If this rendering is adopted a further difficulty arises, for the author of Hebrews seems to place it in the Holy of holies, but Exodus xxx. 6 places it in the holy place. Leonard makes the suggestion that 'As there is mention in Exodus xxx. 10 of an annual expiation by blood on the horns of the altar of incense, this special relation of the altar to the Holy of holies on the great day of Expiation, as well as the fact that it was against the veil of the Holy of holies, may have determined our author to connect the altar of incense by means of the loose expression *which had, echousa*, with the inner sanctuary.'[1] 'Having', the literal meaning of *echousa*, is certainly a loose expression and may mean 'belonging to'. On the great day of atonement the veil or curtain would be drawn, then 'the altar of incense' would in fact be before the mercy seat.

The *ark of the covenant* was a box or chest about four feet long, two and a half feet high and broad (Ex. xxv. 10 ff.). It was overlaid with gold on every side. In the tabernacle and in Solomon's temple there were three treasures within the ark, *the golden pot that had manna* (Ex. xvi. 32–34), *Aaron's rod that budded* (Nu. xvii. 1–11) and *the tables of the covenant* (Ex. xxv. 16 f.; Dt. ix. 9, x. 5). According to Josephus, the Holy of holies of the later temple was completely empty. The *pot* is not stated to be *golden* in the Hebrew but both the LXX and Philo mention that it was golden.

5. On top of the ark was the *mercy seat* and above this were *the cherubims of glory*, which were closely connected with the revelation of God's glory (cf. Ex. xxv. 18–22; Nu. vii. 89; Ezk. x. 19, 20). Between the tables of the law and God's glory was the *mercy seat*, the *hilastērion*. On the great day of atonement the mercy seat was sprinkled with the sacrificial blood (Ex. xxx).

It was not the author's purpose at this time to enter upon a detailed explanation of the symbolism of the tabernacle, although this does not mean that there should be no attempt to explain the symbolism. His mind is on another great aspect of Christ's work—His sacrifice on the cross. Before finally turning his attention to this he discusses the limitations of the priestly ministry of the earthly tabernacle.

6. Although the arrangements of the tabernacle are briefly

[1] *Authorship of the Epistle to the Hebrews*, p. 229.

mentioned, it is made plain that the whole structure was complete, but even so its ministry was spiritually inadequate. This ministry is divided into the daily service of the priests in the holy place and the annual service of the high priest in the Holy of holies.

In their daily service the priests would light the lamps every evening and trim them every morning (Ex. xxvii. 20, 21, xxx. 7 ff.). They would renew the twelve loaves of bread every sabbath (Lv. xxiv. 5 ff.) and burn incense on the golden altar at the time of the morning and evening sacrifice (Ex. xxx. 7, 8). The holy place was nevertheless the scene of man's worship, for the priests represented the worshipper and officiated, however inadequately, in his stead.

7. Only the high priest had access to the Holy of holies but this was limited to *once every year*, i.e. on the day of atonement. Leviticus xvi. 12–16 suggests that he entered at least twice on that day, once with the blood of his own sin offering and then with that for the people. The lawful way into this most holy place was through the blood from the sacrifices which were offered in the outer court. *Prospherei* is present tense, therefore 'offers' (RSV) is more correct that *offered* (AV). Some have suggested that it was the blood which was offered in the most holy place year by year. The most serious objection to this theory is the fact that, though minute directions concerning the ceremonial of the day of atonement are given in Leviticus xvi, the word 'offering' is never associated with the most holy place. The act of sprinkling the blood on and before the mercy seat is never stated to be an act of offering in the Old Testament. Moffatt is right when he says, 'Even the high priest dare not enter without blood (Lev. xvi. 14 f.), i.e. without carrying in blood from the sacrifice offered for his own and the nation's errors.' Year by year the offerings took place at the altar of burnt offerings, and part of the blood of these offerings which the high priest took into the most holy place and sprinkled on and before the mercy seat must be identified with the efficacy

of the sacrifices offered, rather than with the sacrifices themselves. This is illustrated in Leviticus xvi. 3 which commands
Aaron to 'come into the holy place: with a young bullock for
a sin offering, and a ram for a burnt offering'. Now, as this
cannot be taken literally, the high priest must have entered
with the efficacy of the sacrifice of the sin-offering, and as he
entered with blood this must be identified with the efficacy of
the sacrifice.

The second offering on that great day was offered *for the
errors of the people*. 'For the ignorances' would be a more literal
translation; but *agnoēmatōn* is used in a wider sense than
'ignorances' in the LXX. Here it is most probably used as a
general name for sins. Calvin says, 'No sin is free from error or
ignorance, for however knowingly or wilfully any one may sin,
yet it must be that he is blinded by his lust so that he does not
judge rightly, or rather, he forgets himself and God; for men
never deliberately rush headlong into ruin, but being en-
tangled in the deceptions of Satan they lose the power of
judging rightly.'

8. The Levitical ritual was prescribed by God and given to
Moses through the guidance of the Holy Spirit. This was
emblematical, and the true meaning is to be found in the
illumination of the Holy Spirit given here. 'There is a divine
meaning both in the words of Scripture and in the ordinances
of worship' (Westcott).

If *the holiest* refers to the second part of the earthly tabernacle, that is to the Holy of holies, then *the first tabernacle* must
refer to the holy place into which the priests could enter and
from which the people were excluded. The meaning would
then be that so long as the people were excluded from the holy
place, the Holy Ghost signified that the way into God's
presence had not been revealed. If, however, it possesses a
higher meaning, and *the holiest of all* refers directly to God's
presence, then *the first* must refer not to 'the holy place' but to
the whole of the earthly tabernacle. In this case the meaning

would appear to be that while the tabernacle and, subsequently, the temple *was yet standing* the Holy Spirit signified that it was not permitted to enter God's presence. Moffatt thinks that *echein stasin, was yet standing,* is a good Greek phrase for 'to be in existence'. Ronald Knox has 'as long as the former tabernacle maintained its standing', and as originally *stasis* meant 'a standing' this is to be preferred. For the author the old covenant was finished, the veil had been rent, the way was open to *the holiest of all* and men could now draw near to God. The fact that the temple was still in use in Jerusalem made no difference, for it had been rejected by God, and so possessed no authoritative standing.

9, 10. It was the earthly tabernacle which was a type of the heavenly tabernacle, *a figure* or 'symbol' *for the time then present. Eis, for,* with the accusative has the same meaning as its use in the phrase *eis telos,* 'unto the end' (Mk. xiii. 13). The tabernacle and, subsequently, the temple, was a symbol until the new covenant was established. It has been suggested that *kairos, time,* means 'crisis' in this passage as it is chosen in preference to the more general terms *chronos,* 'time', and *aiōn,* 'age'. In this case the earthly tabernacle would be a figure until the crisis at the time of writing which reached its climax in AD 70.

Kath'hēn should be translated 'according to which'; but as it refers not to 'figure' but to the tabernacle, the phrase *in which were offered* conveys the correct meaning. The sacrifices which were offered within the precincts of the tabernacle provided ceremonial purity for the worshippers but were unable to give inward cleansing from which peace of conscience is derived. The use of *suneidēsin, conscience,* points to man as a spiritual, reasonable being, accountable to God, the moral Governor of the universe. It is this responsibility and consciousness of guilt that convinced *him that did the service* (i.e. the worshipper, for the priest officiated instead of the worshipper), that the outward observances of the tabernacle could not remove the guilt of sins. These outward ordinances through their relation to the flesh were imperfect and were imposed for only a limited period—*until the time of reformation*, i.e. until the 'more excellent' covenant which rested upon 'better promises' was established.

Manson asks the question, 'Were the readers a Jewish-Christian group who, for one reason or another, were opposing the ritual freedom of the larger Church? If so', he continues, 'it would be possible to find in these regulations about food and drink the real point at which, and the genuine reason for which, they were holding on sentimentally to the Jewish rites and means of grace.'

iv. A more detailed description of the better ministry (ix. 11–28). Christ's character and the efficacy of the High-Priestly ministry and the sacrificial Victim are discussed (13, 14). Then the necessity of Christ's death to establish the new covenant of which He is Mediator is indicated (15–23). Finally, the superiority of Christ's ministry is seen in the completeness and permanence of its efficacy (24–28).

11. In our Lord's day the Jewish hierarchy's attitude towards the Messiah was political rather than spiritual, national rather than universal. They looked for a Messiah who would overthrow their political enemies, restore their national independence and set up His kingdom within the house of Israel and in the land of Palestine. They failed to perceive that before the restoration of all things the barrier between the all-holy God and sinful man had to be removed. They also failed to realize that it was necessary for the Messiah to come on the scene as High Priest and Victim, so that, by offering Himself as the perfect offering for sin, He could fulfil the divine conditions for the inauguration of the new covenant and, having passed through the greater and more perfect tabernacle, bestow those spiritual and eternal blessings which could meet man's deepest need. For *things to come* some important MSS have 'things that have come', and Nairne maintains that authority, grammar and context combine for the defence of this latter reading; but Moffatt prefers *things to come*. The point is not important, for the new order of things has begun and the blessings associated with it can through faith be experienced now, though the full realization of the good things will come only when faith gives place to sight and the limitations of time have ceased to be.

12. A further illustration from the day of atonement is now brought forward to show that our great High Priest was not limited by the imperfect ordinances of the Levitical system. The high priests first sacrificed the *calves*, or 'young bulls' for their own sins (Lv. xvi. 11), and then offered the *goats* for the sins of the people (Lv. xvi. 15). By the blood of these sacrifices they entered into the Holy of holies. As Christ was without sin He had no need to offer for His own sins; for the sins of the people He offered Himself and *by* (or 'through' or 'in virtue of') *his own blood he entered in once into the holy place.* The RV has, correctly, 'through his own blood', but the RSV has, incorrectly, 'taking . . . his own blood'. In a marginal note this latter version rightly points out that the Greek word *dia* means 'through' and in verses 11 and 14, where this preposition also occurs, uses 'through' in both cases. 'Through' therefore should be used here, and 'taking' or 'with', which are misleading, should be rejected. On the day of atonement when the high priest entered the Holy of holies he took with him material blood, and when our author refers to such an incident he does not use the preposition *dia* but *en*. Our great High Priest, by the sacrifice of Himself, made the final and perfect offering for sin, and on the ground of this all-perfect expiation made through His blood, He entered into God's presence. It is the perfection of this atonement which is the ground of His exaltation and of His unlimited power to save to the uttermost. The gross and crude conception of Christ taking His blood was not in the author's mind, and he is careful to avoid this by his use of *dia*. The fact of the resurrection and exaltation shows that the offering of Himself on the cross had already been accepted by God the Father.

In contrast to the yearly repeated entrances of the high priest into the Holy of holies Christ *entered in once* and for all time. He had a permanent abiding place in the presence of God, a position never obtained by the high priests of the old covenant. *The holy place* here is not the first part of the tabernacle but the second, i.e. the Holy of holies.

Moulton suggests that only the context can decide whether the phrase *having obtained* is antecedent or coincident in places where the participle stands second. Here the context is in favour of antecedent action, for it was through His sacrifice on the cross that eternal redemption was secured. According to Delitzch, 'After He obtained eternal redemption would not be ungrammatical', and Moule thinks a tolerable sense is yielded 'if the action referred to in the participle is viewed as preceding that of the main verb'.[1] Unlike the temporary effect of the offerings on the day of atonement, the redemption obtained is complete and eternal, and thus gives a sense of security to the believer.

13, 14. The author leaves us in no doubt that though the efficacy of the ceremonial offerings in the outward sphere was strictly limited, yet it was effective in this sphere. *The blood of bulls and of goats* was adequate in expiating ceremonial guilt but inadequate in expiating moral guilt. The sprinkling of *the ashes of an heifer* upon *the unclean* was sufficient to remove ceremonial pollution usually acquired through contact with a dead body, which excluded the offender from mingling with God's people in the solemnities of God's service (cf. Nu. xix. 22). Yet it could not remove spiritual defilement. Thus, although the effectiveness of these ceremonial offerings is made plain, their limitations are clearly revealed—they failed to remove the guilt of sin and provide inward cleansing. It is

[1] *An Idiom-book of New Testament Greek*, p. 100.

Christ's blood which purges the conscience of moral guilt and provides the forgiveness which gives the guilty sinner peace. It also cleanses continually from all defilement, thus enabling the sanctified believer to have fellowship with the living God (1 Jn. i. 7).

Three reasons are given why the blood of Christ has such unique significance.

First, Christ offered Himself *through the eternal Spirit*. This translation of the AV suggests a reference to the third Person of the Trinity, but the more probable meaning of the Greek is 'through (His) eternal spirit'. Spirit here is used in opposition to 'flesh' which is outward, material and transitory. Christ offered Himself through the virtue of His eternal spiritual nature, which made the offering of infinite value, and accomplished eternal redemption. 'Christ offered Himself once, and the single sacrifice needed no repetition, since it possessed absolute eternal value as the action of One who belonged to the eternal order' (Moffatt). Second, the sacrifice of Christ was rational and voluntary. *He offered himself.* It was not the slaughter of an unconscious, reluctant victim but an intelligent act of the highest spiritual obedience towards God (Phil. ii. 8), and an act of the highest spiritual love towards man (2 Cor. v. 14, 15). Third, *He offered himself without spot to God.* The author has already discussed the perfect High Priest; he now presents the spotless Victim. The spotlessness is not outward, as in the Levitical sacrifices, but inward and ethical; for Christ's character was blameless throughout His earthly life. 'Christ's offering of Himself without spot to God had an absolute or ideal character. It was something beyond which nothing could be, or could be conceived to be, as a response to God's mind and requirements in relation to sin. It was the final response, a spiritual response, to the divine necessities of the situation.'[1] In the light of these stupendous facts the writer exclaims, *how much more shall the blood of Christ . . . purge* (or cleanse) *your conscience from dead works to serve the living God?*

[1] Denney, *The Death of Christ* (Tyndale Press), p. 129.

15[1]**.** By offering Himself once for all by the blood which He shed, and by the eternal redemption which He secured, Christ has become the Mediator of the new covenant in order that they, who have been called, may have the assured possession of the promised *eternal inheritance. They which are called* includes all the spiritual people of God under the old and new covenants. The patriarchs died, not having received the promises. Their descendants under the old order received the promised earthly inheritance, but did not fully receive those spiritual promises which belong to eternity. Such promises, because they are associated with the spiritual world, are not illusory, for the believer can experience them in time; yet because they belong to the eternal order they are outside the corruptions and defilements of time. Before such promises could be fully realized in the lives of those who are called it was essential that a *redemption of the transgressions that were under the first testament* should be effected. No provision was made under the law to expiate those transgressions committed against the divine will as revealed in His law, which drew upon the transgressor the judicial displeasure of God.

The meaning of *redemption* can be rightly understood only by careful consideration of its sacrificial background. Exodus vi. 6 and xv. 13 refer to the redemption of Israel from the bondage of Egypt, and Leviticus xxv and xxvii to the redemption of property or person from mortgage by the payment of the required price. Yet the association of the word with 'blood' in verses 13 and 14, and with 'without spot to God' in verse 14, shows an inseparable link with the sacrificial 'lamb without blemish and without spot'. To redeem the people of God from the transgressions under the first covenant and bring them into fellowship with God it was necessary for the Lamb of God to die. Death is the penalty of a violated law, 'for the wages of sin is death' (Rom. vi. 23), and it was imperative that this law, which sprang from the perfection of God's character and His

---

[1] There are obscurities throughout verses 15–23 in the av translation. Readers, therefore, are advised to follow the rsv which is much clearer.

moral government, should be honoured. Christ by His death has honoured all the claims of God; He has borne the consequences of man's sin. By His perfect expiation of transgressions He has opened the way for all to receive the promised inheritance.

16, 17. In biblical texts the Greek word *diathēkē, testament,* generally means 'covenant'; but in the papyri and contemporary Hellenistic Greek it possessed a juristic sense and meant 'will'.[1] In these verses it is used by the author in this latter sense. A covenant is an arrangement between related parties and does not necessarily presuppose death, though death almost universally became associated with it. A will is an arrangement of possessions, and has force only when the death of the person who made the will has been established. By this use of a truth of universal application the necessity of Christ's death is demonstrated. It was essential for Christ to die if the promised inheritance (verse 15) was to pass to the believer. The illustration cannot be pressed too far, for, after all, Christ is not dead but alive.

18–20. The author now reverts to the more general meaning attached to *diathēkē* in biblical sources. The first, or Mosaic, covenant was not inaugurated without blood, i.e. without death taking place. The reference is to the description of the sacrifices at the establishment of the covenant given in Exodus xxiv. 3–8, but the author, with his characteristic freedom, has variations

[1] Deissmann has insisted that it should always have this meaning wherever it is found, and the fact that in classical Greek the word for 'covenant' is not *diathēkē* but *sunthēkē* gives added support to his point of view. A closer examination of *sunthēkē*, however, reveals that it always means a 'covenant between two parties coming together on equal terms'. No such covenant could exist beween God and man, and it is possible that for this reason the inspired writers always used *diathēkē*. Another factor which must be considered is that any covenant decreed by God cannot require the death of a testator, and this tells against the invariable use of the word 'will'. It is not unfair to say that it has now been admitted that *diathēkē* can mean either 'covenant' or 'will', yet in our Epistle the latter meaning is confined to these two verses.

in some of the details. After *every precept* had been proclaimed to the people (an action which was in harmony with the law received from God), Moses *took the blood of calves and of goats . . . and sprinkled both the book, and all the people*. The Exodus passage does not mention the sprinkling of the book of the covenant which Moses took into his hands to read, nor does it mention the sprinkling of the vessels of the ministry (see below).

This is the blood of the testament ('covenant') is nearer to the words used by our Lord at the institution of the Lord's Supper than it is to the words 'behold the blood' used by Moses. Yet Moffatt is right when he says, 'Here as throughout the Epistle he ignores the passover or eucharist. As a non-sacerdotal feast, the passover would not have suited his argument.'

21. It would appear from this verse that at the time of the inauguration of the old covenant Moses *sprinkled with blood both the tabernacle, and all the vessels*; but when Moses proclaimed the law which the people promised to obey (Ex. xxiv) the tabernacle was not in existence. Exodus xl, which gives an account of the erection and establishment of the tabernacle, makes no mention of its being sprinkled with blood, but does mention an anointing with oil. Josephus, however, mentions this blood sprinkling when describing this dedication.

22. It was a fixed principle of the law that, almost without exception, all things were purified by blood, and that *without shedding of blood* there was no redemption. This may be a reference to the blood which was poured out at the altar of sacrifice. Yet, even so, the author, his thinking no doubt influenced by the Lord's words, 'this is my blood of the covenant, which is poured out for many for the forgiveness of sins' (Mt. xxvi. 28, RSV), is still concerned with the new covenant ratified by Christ's shed blood, which guarantees forgiveness to those who accept the conditions. The word *schedou*, *almost*, which logically belongs to *ta panta*, *all things*, should be construed with both parts of the sentence. The limitation of the first part is found in Numbers xxxi. 22–24, where fire and water are used for purification, and the limitation of the second is found in Leviticus v. 11–13, where the offering of a tenth part of an ephah of fine flour for a sin-offering brings forgiveness.

23. It is hardly conceivable that *ta epourania, the heavenly things*, refers to the place of God's presence. Job xv. 15 does mention that 'the heavens are not clean in his sight', but the reference is most probably to the material heavens. Moffatt thinks that, when the author suggests that the sacrifice of Christ had to purify heaven itself, the idea becomes almost fantastic. But it is not necessary to assume that the author had such an idea in mind. By assuming a zeugma it is possible, as some suggest, to change the verb 'purified' so that it has the meaning 'consecrated' or 'dedicated'. But it is better to suppose, as Westcott seems to suggest, that *ta epourania* was deliberately chosen to signify not so much heaven itself, as the spiritual sphere in which atonement becomes a reality to the believer. A similar interpretation of the phrase is given in Ephesians and Colossians. Tasker puts forward a similar point of view when he says, 'by entering heaven the crucified Saviour transfers from an earthly localized realm into a spiritual universal sphere the benefits of His passion. Therefore His blood can be thought of as sprinkled in the hearts and consciences of all believers, who are in consequence able to draw nigh, and who do draw nigh unto God through Him'.[1]

24. The earthly sanctuary of the old covenant is compared with the heavenly sanctuary of the new. As the high priest on the day of atonement entered into the Holy of holies, so Christ entered the heavenly Holy of holies through His final, complete and all-sufficient sacrifice. It does not say that He entered God's *presence* to offer His sacrifice, for this had already been done when He offered Himself to God on the cross, but that He is visibly present *for us*, or 'on our behalf'. Leonard

[1] Tasker, p. 37.

rightly says, 'In reality the idea that Christ officiates before the throne of God by any sort of liturgical action or by any active pleading of His passion is nowhere to be found in the Epistle to the Hebrews. . . . We are simply told that He has gone into heaven itself to appear before God on our behalf, . . . and that He is able to save in perpetuity all who come through Him to God, always living to intercede for them.'[1] He is there as the representative of His people, and thus reinstates humanity in God's presence. He is also the great intercessor of all believers, ever making intercession for them and presenting their cause before their heavenly Father.

25, 26. The comparison is now extended to contrast the Levitical high priests and the sacrifices which they continually offered, with the great High Priest and the sacrifice which He offered once for all. The high priest of the old covenant entered into the Holy of holies *with blood of others* or 'with blood not his own' (RSV). The sacrifice demanded was 'without spot', and the high priest, being far from spotless, could not offer himself. Yet because of sin he needed a sacrifice whereby his sins could be forgiven. Christ needed no such sacrifice for 'He knew no sin'; and thus being 'without spot', He could offer Himself for our sins. The purpose of His manifestation at the end of the age was to put away sin by the sacrifice of Himself. That this sacrifice was complete and final is proved by the fact that He died once only. If a repeated offering were necessary for each successive age, then there would have been many incarnations and many deaths. As it is, there was only one incarnation and one death, which is sufficient proof that a full atonement has been made; sin has been *put away* (cf. note on vii. 18).

27, 28. A further illustration is given to prove the finality of Christ's work. In history a man is born, lives and dies but once, and nothing remains but *the judgment* of God. An account

[1] Leonard, p. 73.

of his life must be given to God who will pronounce judgment. So Christ was born, lived and died *once*, and this can never be repeated. He does not await the judgment of God, for His resurrection is proof that God has vindicated His claims. His work of redemption, therefore, is not a failure, for God's seal is upon it. His next appearance on earth will not be related to sin and atonement but to the positive aspects of salvation. The believer through Christ's death has already been saved from the guilt and power of sin, but at the parousia he will be received into eternal life and receive an eternal inheritance, because Christ at His first appearance took upon Himself the consequences and responsibilities of man's sin.

c. The superiority of Christ's sacrifice (x. 1–18)

As the author draws his theological discussion to a close, he recapitulates former truths and makes certain additions to bring out the superiority of Christ's sacrifice over the ritual system of the old covenant. The sacrifices of the old covenant, though many, were inadequate. Christ's sacrifice, though one, was fully adequate (1–4). Animal sacrifices could never fulfil God's will; yet only by the fulfilment of His will could sin be put away. Christ accomplished this (5–10). The high priests stood continually as servants in the holy place, for their work was not finished. The great High Priest sits in God's presence, for by the one offering of Himself He has finished His work (11–14). Scripture testifies that there is no further need of offerings for sin (15–18).

1. The law contains a shadowy outline *of good things to come*. Its sacrificial system reminded the Israelites of sin and revealed the need of atonement, and thus prepared the way for the higher revelation of grace in the gospel. By forbidding the sinner to enter God's presence and yet allowing the high priest to enter once a year, it kept alive the sense of the holiness of God and also the hope of access into His presence. Yet because *the law* contained but *a shadow*, however useful it may

have been, there is found in its system an unceasing repetition of sacrifices which bears witness to the impotency of the old covenant to perfect the worshippers and bring them near to God.

2. If the worshipper had been truly cleansed from his sins, he *should have had no more conscience* (or consciousness) *of sins*, and there would be no further need of sacrifice. The repetition of sacrifice, however, shows that consciousness of sins remains. Therefore the worshipper is not cleansed; he is not made perfect.

3. Although the sacrifices of the old covenant could not remove sins, they could recall them to remembrance so that public notice had to be taken of them. Numbers v. 11–15, which calls the sacrifice of jealousy 'an offering of memorial, bringing iniquity to remembrance', may have influenced the author. *Anamnēsis*, a remembrance, is used by our Lord at the institution of the Last Supper, and many commentators find a contrast between the words of our text and *eis tēn emēn anamnēsin*, 'this do in remembrance of me'. The old covenant sacrifices recalled to mind sins and their responsibility. The remembrance of Christ, the one final, complete and perfect sacrifice, brings to believers' minds the new covenant which He established, and its fundamental blessing: '(thy) sins and . . . iniquities will I remember no more'.

4. Any value which *the blood of bulls and of goats* possessed was relative and typical. It was necessary at the time and fulfilled certain purposes, but *it (was) not possible* that animal blood of this nature *should take away sins*. 'From the spiritual point of view', Berkhof remarks, 'these sacrifices were typical of the vicarious sufferings and death of Christ, and obtained forgiveness and acceptance with God only as they were offered in true repentance, and with faith in God's method of salvation. They had saving significance only in so far as they fixed the attention of the Israelite on the coming Redeemer and the promised redemption.'[1]

5, 6. Psalm cx was used to show the superiority of the priesthood of Christ over the Levitical priesthood. Jeremiah xxxi was quoted to indicate that the covenant of Sinai was superseded by the better covenant; and Psalm xl is now employed to prove that the sacrifice of a rational and spiritual being is more excellent than the sacrifice of dumb creatures.

Wherefore, because the law was ineffective, or in accordance with the impossibility declared in verse 4, *when he cometh into the world,* or 'at His entrance into the world', *he saith,* i.e. Christ Himself speaks from Psalm xl. 6–8.

There are frequent references in the Epistle which make it plain that the author conceived the sacrifice of Christ on the cross as man's only hope. When, therefore, he quotes, *Sacrifice and offering thou wouldest not,* declaring that God had no pleasure in burnt offerings and sin offerings, there is no suggestion that sacrifice was abolished in favour of obedience. The author objects to the substitution of these sacrifices for personal obedience and service. God had no pleasure in a sacrifice of dumb animals which was unaccompanied by the repentance, faith and self-dedication of the offerer. 'The writer's purpose', says Vincent Taylor, 'is not to assert that obedience is better than sacrifice but to claim that, in that it fulfilled the will of God, Christ's sacrifice of Himself surpassed and superseded the Levitical sacrifices.'[2]

Following his usual custom, the author prefers the LXX 'a body hast thou prepared me' to the Hebrew 'ears hast thou digged for me'. Exodus xxi. 6 and Deuteronomy xv. 17 refer to the boring of a slave's ear; if after seven years' service he preferred to remain permanently with his master, the bored ear was a symbol of his willing obedience. For this reason it has been suggested that those who translated the LXX from the Hebrew regarded 'a body hast thou prepared me' as equiva-

[1] *Systematic Theology,* p. 365.   [2] *The Atonement in the New Testament,* p. 177.

lent to the Hebrew 'ears hast thou digged for me'. It appears, however, to be a free interpretation of the original which stated that God has given the Psalmist ears to give heed to God's command. In the context of this verse death is associated with God's command, and since a human body was the only instrument that could truly meet the needs of the situation, a body was prepared for Christ.

7. When the deeper knowledge of the divine will had been revealed and the fulness of time had come, then Christ said *Lo, I come*, or 'Lo, I have come' (RSV). Christ's submission to the Father's will was not only an act of time but was also a process of eternity. *Kephalis, volume,* refers to the knob at the end of the roller around which the manuscript roll was wound; *in the volume of the book* is therefore better translated 'in the roll of the book'. In Psalm xl the reference was to the divine law; but for Christ the meaning is extended to cover all the Old Testament Scriptures.

8–10. *Above when he said* is a reference to Christ's opening words of declaration in verse 5. A twofold action of God was necessary before Christ could fulfil the Father's will. A body must be prepared (5) and the old system must be taken away or deprived of its validity. Before the incarnation Christ had knowledge of the ineffectiveness of the sacrificial system of the law. He also knew that the fulfilment of the will of God meant suffering and death. He was willing and ready to offer Himself as a sacrifice for sins to carry out the redeeming will of God. It is the atonement, therefore, which gives meaning to the incarnation and not the latter to the former. The incarnation was a necessary means to an end, and the end was the putting away of the sin of the world by the offering of the body of Christ.

In the divine will which Christ fulfilled, by *the offering of* His *body . . . once for all, we are sanctified,* or 'we have been consecrated'. Believers have been brought into that true relationship which makes them eternally fit to have fellowship with God and be constituted a worshipping people of God. 'The thought of Christians', Westcott says, 'as included in the Father's will, which Christ fulfilled, corresponds with St. Paul's thought of Christians being "in Christ", an expression which is not found in the Epistle.'

11, 12. To emphasize further the superiority of Christ's one sacrifice on the cross over the many sacrifices of the Jewish priests, an impressive contrast is made between the position of Christ and that of the Levitical priests. The earthly priests were not allowed to sit during their daily ministrations—their work being unfinished. But Christ, the great High Priest, sits on the throne having completed on earth the work which He came to do. Some commentators have suggested that *for ever* should be linked with *one sacrifice for sins*, while others connect it with *sat down*. Westcott remarks that 'the connexion with *sat down* obscures the idea of the perpetual efficacy of Christ's one sacrifice; it weakens the contrast with *hestēke, standeth*; it imports a foreign idea of the assumption (*ekathisen*) of royal dignity by Christ'. This statement is far too sweeping, for the abiding efficacy of the one sacrifice is expressed in verse 14 and the manifest antithesis seems to be between the priests standing daily offering their imperfect sacrifices and Christ sitting *for ever* having offered the one perfect sacrifice. Knox, following the mistranslation of the Vulgate which led to the strange theory of Christ pleading His passion in heaven, translates: Christ 'sits for ever at the right hand of God, offering for our sins a sacrifice that is never repeated'. He rightly corrects this in the margin by referring to the Greek, which he translates: Christ 'has atoned for our sins and taken His seat at the right hand of God'.

The use of *perielein, take away,* likens sin to a robe which has wrapped itself around man, and which must be stripped off, just as the ceremonial of the law required the removal and washing of the garments of the unclean (cf. note on xii. 1).

13. I Corinthians xv. 22 ff. suggests that Christ's enemies are to be destroyed after His return; but here the suggestion seems to be made that from the time Christ sits on the throne until the parousia He waits until His enemies are destroyed. Paul had in mind the final victory of Christ over the devil and the supernatural powers of evil, but the author of the Epistle to the Hebrews conceives Christ's battle as won; all that He waits for being supreme dominion.

14. There is a contrast between the law with its priesthood and many sacrifices which failed to bring perfection (vii. 11, 19, x. 1) and the one offering of Christ which has done all that is required. Through faith this perfect work becomes a living and effective reality in those *that are sanctified* or 'are being sanctified', i.e. in those whose moral and spiritual experience is still progressing to its full realization. *Them that are sanctified*, however, may be iterative and mean 'those who from age to age receive sanctification'.

15-18. As if the witness of Christ found in Psalm xl. 6-8 was not sufficient, the author strengthens his position by the introduction of a further witness—the Holy Spirit who through the Scriptures (Je. xxxi. 31-34, already referred to in viii. 8 ff.) testifies that there is no further need of offering for sin.

The word of prophecy spoke of the crowning promise of the new covenant, namely, forgiveness of sins. The Scriptures also testified that the precise object of sacrifice was to make forgiveness of sins possible—'without shedding of blood is no remission'. Through the sacrifice of Christ the new covenant has been established; therefore God no longer remembers sins and iniquities. Consequently, if sin is removed for ever, there is no necessity for any further sacrifice. 'Henceforth', writes Stibbs, 'there is no longer any place for any kind of offering for sin or presentation before God of Christ's one sin offering. Reconciliation has not to be made or completed by any further propitiatory offering or memorial of Christ's sacrifice; it has simply to be received by penitent faith as an already complete and available benefit of the finished work of Christ (see Rom. v. 11, RV)'.[1]

VII. EXHORTATION AND ADMONITION
(x. 19–xii. 29)

The author now dwells upon some practical consequences of the theological arguments of the earlier chapters (x. 19–39), and upon the characteristics and triumphs of faith (xi. 1–40). An exhortation follows, culminating in a vision of the Church and the heavenly kingdom (xii. 1–29).

a. Privileges and responsibilities (x. 19–39)

The author passes from argument to earnest exhortation (19–25), after which he pauses to give a solemn warning (26–31). He then returns again to appeal and encouragement (32–39).

19. The structure of this appeal is the same as that in iv. 14–16, but in the intervening sections the great doctrine of Christ's eternal priesthood, and its connection with His heavenly ministry and His one perfect sacrifice, has been expounded and established by conclusive arguments. The effectiveness of this aspect of Christ's work is now shown to lie in the liberty of the believer to enter God's presence in contrast to those under the old covenant who had no direct access to God; and even the privilege granted to the high priest to approach Him on their behalf was confined to one day a year. The believer can approach the holiest not only without fear and trembling but with full assurance that *by the blood of Jesus*, i.e. in virtue of Christ's better sacrifice, he will be graciously received by the Father.

20. This access into God's presence has been *consecrated* or

[1] *The New Bible Commentary* (Inter-Varsity Fellowship), p. 1105.

opened up *for us . . . by a new and living way. Prosphatos, new,*
which is found only here in the New Testament, originally
meant 'fresh killed'; but the second element in this dropped
out of use and the word came to be used generally for what
was 'new', 'fresh' or 'recent', without any sacrificial allusion.
Here it has the meaning of a way newly opened which before
was inaccessible, for even the believer of the Old Testament
could not enter God's presence freely and openly, nor with the
joyful confidence and intimacy suggested in this passage. This
newly opened way is *living*, or effective, for the living Lord is
Himself the way (Jn. xiv. 6). Unlike the ineffective way of
senseless animals and dead works of the old covenant, or 'a
lifeless pavement trodden by the high priest', our great High
Priest has opened this way for us *through the veil, that is to say,
his flesh.* This metaphorical phraseology must in some way be
associated with the curtain which in the tabernacle separated
the holy place from the Holy of holies (cf. ix. 3). When Christ
died on the cross the veil was rent in the midst signifying that
the old form of ceremonial religion had ceased, or had been
rejected by God. The identification of the *veil* with Christ's
flesh has created a difficulty and to overcome this some commentators connect *flesh* not with *veil* but with the *new and living
way*. In this case the words become descriptive of the manner
in which Jesus, by the offering of Himself, opened a way
through the veil. It seems more natural, however, to identify
flesh with the *veil* which had to be rent to bring to an end the
old covenant. It was necessary for Christ's flesh to be rent so
that the blood might be poured out to establish the new
covenant. Also by His death the barrier of sin was removed,
and a greater and clearer revelation of God was made possible.
As Tasker trenchantly says, 'His death, as it were, uncovered
God so that man might have a vision of the glory that shone
upon His face.'[1]

21. The thought is now very close to that found in iii. 1–6

[1] Tasker, p. 30.

and iv. 14. *Having an high priest*, i.e. since we have a great High Priest, a royal Priest and a priestly King who is *over the house of God*. It is unnecessary to limit *the house of God* to the Church triumphant or to the Church militant, for it includes all God's people whether under the old covenant or the new (cf. iii. 2–4).

22. In the exhortation now given, liturgical phrases associated with the old covenant ritual are used; but, as Moffatt rightly points out, this 'does not mean that Christians are priests, with the right of entry in virtue of a sacrifice which they present'. Because to approach God was a priestly prerogative under the older order, the author describes the Christian access to God in sacerdotal metaphors. *Proserchōmetha, let us draw near*, is used of the approach of the Israelites, after ceremonial atonement, to the earthly sanctuary. They did not enter the Holy of holies themselves, however, but only in the person of the high priest who represented them. The believer, without the intervention of any human priest, has direct access to God Himself. Yet his approach must be *with a true heart*, i.e. with perfect sincerity, for *true* has the same meaning here as it has in viii. 2; it suggests that the approach to God should be made without hypocrisy, 'in spirit and in truth'. Yet perfect sincerity is not sufficient; the believer must come *in full assurance of faith*, i.e. in fullness of faith in Christ and in the perfection of His sacrificial work on the cross in virtue of which access is made possible. This faith must not be divided between Christianity and Judaism, or between Christ and the Church, or between our great High Priest, the only and all-sufficient Mediator, and a human priesthood.

The readers are reminded that just as the Jewish priests were purified from ceremonial defilement by being sprinkled with blood (Ex. xxix. 21; Lv. viii. 30) so their own hearts have been sprinkled with the blood of Christ; and the experience of a cleansed conscience gives the sinner the assurance of the removal of guilt and confidence to approach the Holy God.

23. Some commentators connect *and our bodies washed with pure water* with what has gone before in verse 22, but it may be a parenthetic clause having the same relationship to *let us hold fast the profession* as 'having our hearts sprinkled . . .' has to 'let us draw near'. The believer should draw near to God with firm inner certainty of faith, on the basis of Christ's sacrifice, since he has been sprinkled with blood. In like manner he should hold fast his profession since the bodies of Christians have been washed with pure water. This washing could refer to baptism, which was a symbol of inward purity. The readers had submitted to baptism, which meant that they had publicly proclaimed their renunciation of Judaism. On the other hand, there is little doubt that the author had the Levitical purification in mind (cf. Lv. viii. 6–23; Ex. xxix. 21, xxx. 19–21); where the priests are said to have been washed in water and where they are commanded to wash in the laver before entering the tabernacle. Calvin and others, asserting that the author is referring to the ancient ceremonies of the law, maintain that by water he designates the Spirit of God in accordance with what is said in Ezekiel xxxvi. 25, I will 'sprinkle clean water upon you, and ye shall be clean'.

The second exhortation is to persevere, and so hope is introduced and not *faith* which the AV, without authority, substitutes for 'hope'. The simplicity and spirituality of Christianity no doubt gave rise to much criticism and placed the readers in danger of drifting back to ritualistic and other outward attractions of Judaism. They may have been strongly provoked to let go by the pressing difficulties and urgency of the times. A powerful persuasive encouragement to Christian fidelity is added, *for he is faithful that promised*. Mastery of the true significance of the faithfulness of God to His glorious promises should strengthen the Christian's faithfulness to his confession of hope in the Lord Jesus Christ.

24. The third exhortation urges them to fix their attention not on themselves but on *one another*, and the reason given is

that they might *provoke unto love and to good works*. Their attention was not to be centred wholly on their own individual
salvation, for they belonged to the body of Christ, and as members of this body they had certain responsibilities with regard
to the other members. They were to provoke one another to
love and to good works. *Paroxusmon, provoke,* is more generally
used in a bad sense, with the meaning of 'provocation' or
'exasperation' (cf. Acts xv. 39). It is just possible that their
actions at that time were provoking rather to hatred than to
love. They are, therefore, strongly urged to watch one another,
that in so doing there may be a mutual provocation to love and
Christian faithfulness.

25. The exhortation that the readers should not forsake the
assembling of themselves together arises from what has just
been stated and from man's need as a spiritual being. Yet it
also contains a warning to those who were already leaving the
Christian assembly, for such action implied that they did not
regard Christianity as the complete and final revelation; this
could easily lead to a renunciation of the Christian Church and
faith. The group who were leaving their brethren in the lurch
may have been a small group of teachers, more intelligent than
the rest, as some commentators suggest. But the Epistle as
a whole and the use of *episynagōge,* 'gathering together', are
strongly in favour of the view that these persons were Jewish
Christians who, through fear of the Jews and dread of persecution, had discontinued attending the Christian assemblies.
Whoever they were, their example was not to be followed; on
the contrary, true Christians were to encourage one another
to attend the Christian gatherings. A forceful motive—the
approaching day of crisis—is appended to encourage them to
stand together, and it is made clear that the finest way to proclaim their union publicly was in the common Christian
meeting-place. Primarily, *the day approaching* refers to the
destruction of Jerusalem in AD 70, and the political disturb-
ances of the author's time were strong evidence of its rapid

approach. Yet *the day*, which is the regular term for the day of the Lord, cannot be limited to the catastrophe of AD 70 but includes also the parousia which is ever drawing near. It was not so evident to the early Christians that the parousia and the destruction of Jerusalem were not synchronous.

In verses 26–31 the danger of neglecting the Christian assemblies is more vividly brought out. Such neglect may lead to a forsaking of the Christian Church and a renunciation of the Christian faith. This may be followed by utter contempt of the Son of God and the Spirit of grace.

26, 27. The reason given for the urgency of the above exhortation is found in the words *for if we sin wilfully*. . . . This last word, which is placed first in the Greek for emphasis, shows that the deliberate and continual rejection of Christianity is a decision of the will which acts contrary to what one would have expected from the knowledge of the truth which has been received. *Epignōsis, knowledge,* is often taken to mean full or perfect knowledge, but that this is its invariable meaning is very doubtful. The use of the compound verb in the papyri led MM to endorse the conclusion reached by Robinson in his commentary on Ephesians that it does not denote complete or perfect knowledge. They are also doubtful whether the compound noun signifies fuller or more accurate knowledge. Although generally speaking *epignōsis* does not mean knowledge in the abstract, yet its association with the philosophy of the day may have influenced the author to use it in this way. Certainly a clearly formulated system of beliefs would not constitute Christianity as presented in this Epistle. There must also be a personal relation to God in Christ. When the latter experience takes place the believer comes under the new covenant with its promise that God remembers the sins of believers no more. If, therefore, these hypothetical 'apostates' were true believers, then this fundamental blessing of the new covenant is difficult to understand. It is better, therefore, to suppose that the only persons the author can conceive of apostasizing are those who have received Christianity as a formulated system of beliefs, but without any personal experience of God in Christ. Such persons are typified in Balaam and Simon Magus. *The knowledge of the truth*, therefore, would mean that they had discerned and received the truth of Christianity but that it had not become a living force in their lives.

The author is careful not to say that the readers had sinned wilfully, but simply states that if such a thing did happen certain results would inevitably follow. To have understood the significance for themselves of the one sin-offering which God has accepted, and then to reject it deliberately, would be to sin against light and knowledge, and no other sacrifice existed which could be of any assistance to them. On the contrary, there would be left only an alarming anticipation of the judgment; and in this terrible expectation of the wrath of God which burns like fire, the bearing of the consequences of sins would have already begun.

28, 29. Using the exegetical argument from the lesser to the greater, he asks the readers to decide the punishment of the greater sinner. The sentence decreed against the person who *despised*, or set at nought, *Moses' law* was inexorable—*without mercy*. The reference taken from Deuteronomy xvii. 2–7 refers to those who were guilty of the sin of idolatry. They denied the validity and the authority of certain divine ordinances when they transferred their worship from Jehovah to foreign deities. On the ground of the evidence of two or three people they were condemned and no mercy was shown to them.

The author now uses impressive and solemn language to bring out the gravity of wilful rebellion against the Father, Son and Holy Spirit. To trample *under foot* One who is *the Son of God*, the 'Light of Light' and 'very God of very God' is a continuous repudiation of God's final revelation. To count *the blood of the covenant* as *an unholy thing* is a vilification of the atonement through the Son; to treat with scorn the Spirit of grace is to sin against the Holy Spirit. The punishment of a person who has sinned so deeply must be inconceivably severe, and absolutely certain. *The blood . . . wherewith he was sanctified* may refer to Christ who was sanctified to be an eternal High Priest. It more likely refers to the 'apostate' but, as John Owen points out, sanctification in his case would not be real or internal but merely external, for true sanctification implies separation from sin and dedication to God. The omission of the words *wherewith he was sanctified* by the Codex Alexandrinus was most probably due to an attempt to avoid this difficulty.

30. Two quotations from Deuteronomy xxxii. 35, 36 are now introduced to illustrate the awful gravity of the judgment which will fall upon the wilful sinner. The first of these quotations is slightly different from the Hebrew, but more so from the LXX, which is unusual in this Epistle. Paul, when quoting this passage in Romans xii. 19, uses the same words as the author of Hebrews. Some commentators have suggested that both writers used the paraphrase of Onkelos, others that both were using a form of the verse which had become proverbial. Others again have suggested that the writer may have borrowed from Paul.

We know him, i.e. we know who He is and what He can do. He is the living and omniscient God who knows His true people and can sift them from the false. He is the omnipotent God who can defend His people and destroy their enemies and also vindicate His own character.

31. In 2 Samuel xxiv. 14 David prefers to fall into the hand of the Lord rather than into the hand of man; but *to fall into the hands of the living God* is used in a different sense here, referring to the deliberate apostate who falls a victim to the retributive judgment of God.

In verses 32–39 the author follows the same pattern of severe warning succeeded by appeal and encouragement as in vi. 4–6 and vi. 9. The appeal is first of all retrospective—they are to remember their past record; and then prospective—they are to fix their attention on Christ's return, which is imminent.

32, 33. In the early days of their Christian experience the readers had given proof of their Christian constancy and love in the face of uncompromising hostility from the Jews and persecution from the Gentiles. 'The storm burst on them early', says Moffatt; 'they weathered it nobly; why give up the voyage when it is nearly done?' Though *athlēsin, fight,* and *theatrizomenoi, made a gazingstock,* suggest the Roman arena where persons doomed to die were exposed to the gaze and scorn of the crowds, xii. 4 makes it quite clear that their sufferings had not yet resulted in martyrdom.

34. The reading *for ye had compassion of me in my bonds,* if correct, would strongly support the Pauline authorship. There is, however, another reading, *tois desmiois,* 'with the prisoners', which is strongly supported by modern commentators. The Chester Beatty papyrus has *tois desmois,* and this seems at a cursory glance to support the Received Text, but as Kenyon remarks, 'the omission of *mou, my,* renders this very doubtful and suggests the possibility, if not the probability, that the *desmois* of the papyrus is a single scribal error for *desmiois.*'

Not only had the readers suffered physically and mentally, but they had been willing to share the reproaches and afflictions of their persecuted and imprisoned brethren. Their expression of grief at the condition of their brethren developed into practical help, for the true Christian spirit can never remain content with mere words. They had also been ready to suffer cheerfully the loss of property, being fully persuaded that their true and permanent treasure was *in heaven.*

The words *in heaven* are not found in the best and oldest MSS and are an interpretative gloss of the translators. The reading *en heautois, in yourselves,* is also doubtful, being found only in a few minuscules with little authority. There are two variants—

heautois, 'for yourselves' and *heautous*, 'yourselves'. As the best authorities are in favour of the latter it is to be preferred. Some have translated this 'perceiving that you have your own selves as better possessions'; but this is, as Moffatt rightly points out, far too subtle. So convinced were the readers of the truth of Christianity and of their true and permanent possession that they bore joyfully the loss of their material possessions.

35, 36. They are urged, therefore, not to throw off their Christian *confidence* as they would a worthless garment, but to continue to speak and act boldly for Christ as they had so gloriously done in those former days. Such action would not be in vain, for there is a Christian *recompence of reward* which depends not upon any legal right but upon the goodness and faithfulness of God.

The necessity for *patience*, or endurance, is now stressed, for the temptations and trials of that day were exceptionally severe. Before *the promise* can be received *the will of God* must be fulfilled. What God wills or requires has been limited by some to belief in Christ and to confession of Christ before men. Both of these are required, but so also is steadfast perseverance in faith and hope.

37. The need for endurance is only for *mikron, hoson hoson, a little while*. A literal translation of this phrase would be 'a little, how much, how much', i.e. a very, very little time. These words from Isaiah xxvi. 20 are prefaced to the main quotation from Habakkuk. Their use by the author is to show that *he that shall come . . . will not tarry*. His return is imminent. The quotation is adapted from Habakkuk ii. 3, 4 where the prophet speaks of the fulfilment of the prophecy regarding the overthrow of the Chaldaeans. The Hebrew text of this passage makes it plain that it is the vision of approaching salvation which will not tarry, but the LXX introduces a personal aspect. A rescuer is to come. The author follows the LXX, but by inserting the definite article makes it clear that the coming

One is Christ whose return will bring to an end all trials and usher in the promised blessing.

38. The author continues to use the LXX of the prophecy of Habakkuk but makes certain changes. Habakkuk ii. 4 reads, 'If he should draw back, my soul has no pleasure in him, but the righteous one shall live by my faithfulness' or, possibly, 'by faith in me'. These words are now reversed and the pronoun *mou*, 'my' (omitted in the MSS followed by AV), is transferred from after *pisteōs, faith*, to before it, i.e. after *dikaios*, 'righteous', thus reading 'my righteous one shall live by faith'. This title 'righteous one', sometimes used of the Jewish nation and of the Lord Jesus Christ, could here refer to individuals or the community. 'More clearly than anywhere else in the Epistle', says Manson, 'it would appear that disappointment over the delay of the Parousia of Christ was one cause at least of the community's apathy and loss of faith.' Certainly *tis*, *any man*, is not found in the Greek, and is unnecessary, for 'my righteous one' is the subject of both clauses. The righteous one, whether an individual or group, who belongs to God and whose trust continues in God and His promises *shall live*, i.e. he shall survive the present trial and receive his eternal reward. If, however, he *draw back* through fear, God *shall have no pleasure in him*. Calvin takes this last phrase to be an expression of the *author's* feeling, but this is very doubtful.

39. It is now made plain that in his serious warnings against apostasy the author has only been putting forth a hypothetical case. 'Warnings and admonitions are the very means which God employs to secure the final salvation of His people; and to conclude from such warnings that they may finally fall away, is by no means a legitimate argument.'[1]

b. The characteristics and triumphs of faith (xi. 1-40)

In the previous chapter faith is mentioned as the principle of

[1] Calvin, *Commentaries: Hebrews*, editorial note, p. 289.

spiritual life and the impetus of patient endurance. Having quoted the great saying of Habakkuk—'The just shall live by faith'—the writer now proceeds to vindicate its truth, not by a definition of faith in the strictly theological sense, but by a description of its effects (1–6) and by a series of brilliant biographical illustrations (7–40). Thus in a sense his approach could be called a synthesis of the supposed tension between the Pauline thesis, 'the just shall live by faith', and James' antithesis 'by works a man is justified'.

1. The position in the original of *is, estin,* at the beginning of the sentence lays strong emphasis upon the reality of faith and is no mere copula as some suggest. Now this faith, the writer is saying, which we have experienced and of which the prophet wrote is *the substance of things hoped for*. *Substance* can hardly mean reality here, for faith does not bestow reality on things which have no substance or reality in themselves. It may have the same meaning as in iii. 14, making faith the confidence or assurance of things hoped for. MM maintain that in all cases of its use in the papyri there is the same central idea of something which underlies visible conditions and guarantees a future possession. They suggest, therefore, that the essential meaning of Hebrews xi. 1 is 'Faith is the title-deeds of things hoped for'. Thus a man who has true faith possesses the title-deeds of eternal realities, and the conviction and proof that these realities, though unseen, can be a living and effective power in his life.

2, 3. In religious history *the elders*, or venerable fathers, beginning with Abel, were distinguished for this quality of faith which *obtained* for them a *good report*, i.e. they received from God a favourable testimony of their life of faith. Even in the world-history of revelation, beginning with the creation, faith is manifested in its perception of the existence and operation of God, as the unseen Creator and Sustainer of the visible universe and in its perception of the overruling providence of God in world affairs. The suggestion that there is here a reference to the formless void of Genesis i. 2 out of which the present creation was evolved has little to support it. The term *aiōnas* has the same meaning as in i. 2 and, therefore, means 'ages' rather than *worlds*. Vaughan thinks of time-worlds having their periods of duration and their limits of existence; but the thought is rather that of the life of the world in its successive and progressive stages leading to the consummation, or the gathering together in one of all things in Christ.

4. The sacrifice which Abel offered was more acceptable than Cain's, for it was offered in faith. Faith thus makes an important difference; but it is neither suggested nor implied that where faith exists any kind of sacrifice will suffice. There can be no approach to God apart from faith; yet such faith will only please God when it is in harmony with, and responsive to, the truth which God has revealed.

It is difficult to decide whether *faith* or *sacrifice* should be inserted after *by which* and *by it*. In support of 'faith' is the whole context which is a discourse on faith, yet the insertion of 'sacrifice' certainly simplifies the construction. The same difficulty occurs in verse 7 where 'by the which' can refer to either 'faith' or 'the ark'. 'On the whole', Westcott remarks, 'it appears to be most natural to see in the sacrifice the means through which the testimony was borne, and in the faith which prompted the sacrifice that whereby Abel still speaks.'

By the acceptance of Abel's gift God testified that he was righteous; but we are not told how this sacrifice was accepted. Some have suggested that fire came down from heaven and consumed it. It is highly probable that there was an outward visible sign associated with this incident, but there is no record of what it was.

5, 6. The faith of Enoch is brought forward as the second example of the power of faith. The incident is found in Genesis v. 24, and the author adopts his usual custom of following the

LXX which says that Enoch 'was not found, for God translated him'. The Hebrew, however, simply states 'he was not; for God took him', and from this it has been argued that his mode of departure from this life is left open, a statement which cannot be said of the LXX version or of Hebrews. Whether *that he should not see death* be taken as final or quasi-final it cannot alter the sense. Enoch was removed from this scene, as Ronald Knox rightly translates, 'without the experience of death'. This is not the same as John viii. 51 where 'death', like 'life', is viewed as a state. The same Greek phrase is, however, found in Luke ii. 26, where it is recorded that Simeon did not see or experience death until he had seen the Lord's Christ.

'Before Enoch was translated he had this testimony that he pleased God' is the LXX interpretation of the Hebrew 'and Enoch walked with God'. The Scriptures record that Enoch had fellowship with God before they mention his translation. To obtain God's approval and blessing, faith is necessary. Enoch had this faith, for the evidence of his belief in God as a living reality is demonstrated in his communion with God, and God set His seal upon Enoch's belief that He is a rewarder of them that diligently seek Him, by translating him.

Verse 6 is neither confined nor necessarily related to Enoch. It is a truth of universal application that whoever approaches God to worship Him and to receive a blessing from Him must believe in His existence and in His power to recompense those who diligently seek Him.

7. Noah having received a divine communication that certain events, though unseen, would come to pass was moved with godly fear and reverence and prepared an ark for the salvation of himself and household, and thus became an example of faith. The antecedent of *by the which* is not stated. It can, therefore, refer either to *faith* or to 'the preparing of the ark' (cf. verse 4). Whichever reading is preferred the sense is not altered, for whether it be 'by faith' or by his action in 'preparing the ark' the result is the same, namely the condemnation of the world. Vaughan makes the suggestion that as verse 3 dealt with faith in respect of things past, and verses 4 to 6 with faith in respect of the present, so verses 7 ff. deal with it in respect of the future.

In Genesis vi. 9 Noah is called righteous, and in 2 Peter ii. 5 he is styled 'a preacher of righteousness'. He is also associated with righteousness in Ezekiel xiv. 14, Ecclesiasticus cliv. 17 and the Book of Wisdom x. 4. It was by the way of faith that he became an inheritor of righteousness, and though this expression is not exactly the same as Paul's 'righteousness of faith', there is no adequate reason to think that the sense is fundamentally different, though our author does not confine faith to the appropriation of the righteousness which is freely offered in Christ, as Paul so vividly and consistently does.

8–10. Abraham, the father of the faithful, was called to go out of the land of the Chaldaeans in Mesopotamia and into the land of Canaan. He accepted the challenge, and obeyed the call because he trusted God and believed His promises. In Genesis xi. 27 to xii. 5 Terah, the father of Abraham, is associated with this journey, but the divine monition has been given to Abraham (cf. Acts vii. 4 ff.).

Another proof of his enduring faith is seen in his willingness to dwell as a stranger in the land which had been promised to him, without rights or possessions, though eventually he did buy a piece of land for a burying-place. His believing expectation was for things above; therefore he was willing to live as an alien in his own country. Even his accommodation was temporary, for with his children he became a wanderer dwelling in tents ever looking to that *city which hath* firm and permanent *foundations*. The reference here is not to the earthly Jerusalem, as some suggest, but to the heavenly city whose architect and designer is God. This heavenly city became a theme current among the Jews, and the early Church associated it with the return of Christ.

11, 12. *Also* (Gk. *kai*) should be translated here 'even'. Even Sarah, though previously doubting, eventually believed the promises of God; and even though beyond the age of child-bearing she received power from God for the founding of a posterity. Zuntz finds *Sarah* less suited than most to serve as a model of unfailing trust, and maintains that the words *Sarah herself* should be treated as a gloss and Abraham regarded as the subject of the sentence. But surely this is to look at the actions of those who lived in ancient times too much through the eyes of a modern reader. In the genealogy of our Lord three out of the four names of women mentioned are those of Tamar, who played the harlot, Rahab the harlot, and the wife of Uriah who was an adulteress. Such actions may shock us in these 'more enlightened' times, but it cannot be right to judge the actions of those who lived in ancient times by modern standards. Sarah's faith may not have shone like that of some of the other heroes mentioned in this chapter, but considering her great age she had ample reason to doubt. The marvel is that her faith was able to rise above it. Tasker rejects Zuntz's suggestion and points out that the words 'even Sarah herself' may give us the insight we need into the author's thought about Genesis xviii. 'Even Sarah's acceptance of a promise which at first she seemed to hear with indifference is to the mind of the *auctor ad Hebraeos* a venture into the unseen world which faith makes real.'[1] Zuntz is on more solid ground when he maintains that *katabolēn spermatos* refers to a male, for *katabolē* was certainly a technical term for the sowing of seed. Yet *katabolē* may have other meanings, and the translation may be 'she received power to establish a posterity'. MM compare in connection with Hebrews xi. 11 the noun *katabolaios* found in a papyrus with the meaning store-place.

13. The express mention of the promises not given to the antediluvians, and the statement that Enoch should not experience death are strongly in favour of *these all* being confined

[1] *New Testament Studies*, Vol. II, pp. 182, 183.

to Abraham, Sarah, Isaac and Jacob (verses 8–12). To these noble patriarchs the promises had been given, and by faith throughout their lives they looked forward to their fulfilment, and in the way of faith they all died *not having received the promises* in the fuller sense. The eternal realities, however, which God had revealed, they had by the eye of faith perceived *afar off*, and their souls *embraced them* or 'joyfully greeted them'. As the words *and were persuaded of them* add nothing to the sense of the passage and have little manuscript authority, they should be omitted.

They had received a divine call to a spiritual inheritance, and as they journeyed to that inheritance they confessed, or acknowledged, before men that they were sojourners and pilgrims. *Strangers and pilgrims, xenoi parepidēmoi*, are found in conjunction in only two places in the LXX, in Genesis xxiii. 4 where Abraham in his request for a burying-place defines himself as 'a stranger and a sojourner' (RSV), and in Psalm xxxix. 12 where David in his plea for divine help declares himself to be a 'passing guest' in the land and a 'sojourner' as all his fathers were. The technical distinction between the two words is that a *parepidēmos* has acquired certain limited rights through the payment of a tax, but no such distinction is in the author's mind. Nairne likens the patriarchs to nomads on their way to a city across a desert, who descry its towers from a distance but cannot reach it in that day's march; they greet the sight but encamp once more afar off.

14–16. Within the hearts of these patriarchs there was a deep longing for a permanent settlement. Had their longing been for Mesopotamia they could at any time have returned to their native home. Their longing was higher and greater, reaching out to that unseen city 'whose builder and maker is God'. This fine exhibition of faith in eternal realities is acknowledged by *God* who *is not ashamed to be called their God*, and who many years after their departure from this life calls Himself the God of Abraham, Isaac and Jacob (cf. Lk. xx. 37, 38). He also looks upon them as the people destined for that city which He Himself has prepared. 'He might', according to Moffatt, 'have been ashamed to call Himself such, had He not made this provision for their needs and prepared this reward for their faith.'

17, 18. The supreme test of Abraham's faith recorded in Genesis xxii is now introduced with the object of showing the supreme triumph of faith. The AV twice mentions that *Abraham . . . offered up Isaac*, but this hardly does justice to the perfect and imperfect tenses used here. Thumb and Mosely suggest that *prosenēnochen*, 'offered', is aoristic perfect and Moffatt is inclined to this viewpoint. But the extension of the perfect is a strong characteristic of the author, and there seems no adequate reason to reject its use in this passage. Moulton speaks of the incident as an ideally completed action, as permanently recorded in Scripture. *Prospheren, offered*, is a conative imperfect with the meaning 'he was attempting to offer' or 'ready to offer'. Abraham fully intended to offer Isaac, but his intention was never executed—his sacrifice was a bloodless one.

Monogenēs, only begotten, has not the same meaning here as it has in John i. 18; it is simply used as a synonym for *agapētos*, 'beloved'. Both these words are used in the LXX to translate the same Hebrew word meaning 'only'. Abraham had two sons, Ishmael and Isaac, but the latter was the only son of Sarah and the only child of the promises. In him the promise of the inheritance of Canaan, the promise of a countless posterity, and the promise that all nations should be blessed, were to be fulfilled. The test of Abraham's faith lay in the apparent conflict between the promise of God that Isaac was to be heir and the commandment of God that he was to be put to death, which meant the extinction of Abraham's seed and the end of the promise. His faith was equal to the test. Believing that God's promise could not fail, he was convinced that if Isaac died God would raise him from the dead.

19. To account for the statement that Abraham received back Isaac *in a figure*, when in reality he was restored, is not without difficulty. According to the AV the antecedent of *from whence*, *hothen*, can only be *dead*. Isaac was received back from the dead. Yet the invariable use of *hothen* in this Epistle is 'on account of', 'for this reason' (cf. ii. 17, iii. 1, vii. 25, viii. 3, ix. 18). If this is the correct translation, the meaning would be that because Abraham believed that God was able to raise Isaac from the dead he was restored to his father. The real difficulty, however, is in the clause *in a figure*, *en parabolē*. Some have suggested that Abraham believed that God would raise the dead, therefore he *risked* the life of Isaac (a possible meaning of the cognate verb *paraballesthai*) and, in consequence, received him back as a reward. Moreover, *komizo*, is frequently used with the sense of 'receiving something back as a reward'. The RSV has 'figuratively speaking', but if this is all that the author meant, then one would have expected him to use the adverb *parabolōs*, or the expression *hōs epos eipein* as he does in vii. 9. Arndt and Gingrich are probably right in supposing that *en parabolē* implies that the author regarded the incident as a type of the violent death and resurrection of Christ; and in a similar way Knox interprets the passage 'Abraham received his son from the dead, inasmuch as his life was spared unexpectedly, "in a hidden sense", because the sacrifice of Isaac was a type of our Lord's crucifixion.' Abraham's faith was able to reach the wonderful heights of the resurrection and for this reason Isaac was restored to him as one from the dead, as a type of the death and resurrection of the divine Son who was not spared (cf. Rom. viii. 32; Jn. viii. 56).

20. It was *by faith* that Isaac blessed his two sons, Jacob and Esau. The author makes it clear that it was the *things to come*, or 'the unseen things of the future', especially the pre-eminence of Jacob, that Isaac perceived by faith, but it is difficult to gather where Isaac's faith was exercised from the incident recorded in Genesis xxvii. His natural desire and intention had been to bless Esau, his firstborn, but as Jacob supplanted Esau of his birthright so he supplanted him of his blessing. His faith may have been evident at the time when he grasped the fact that Jacob had deceived him, for he refused to withdraw the blessing, perceiving in it the overruling providence of God. It was Jacob and not Esau who perceived the value of spiritual blessings, and Genesis xxv. 23 makes it clear that it was according to God's will that the elder should serve the younger, i.e. it was in Jacob that the promises were to be fulfilled.

21. *By faith Jacob, when he was dying, blessed* Ephraim and Manasseh; yet in the record given of this in Genesis xlviii there is a marked deference paid to Ephraim, the younger. The sons are made to correspond with Reuben and Simeon, and Ephraim became an alternative name for the northern kingdom of Israel. The Hebrew word *matteh, staff*, originally had no vowels and, therefore, could just as easily be pointed *mittah*, 'bed'. The LXX which is followed here has *and he died leaning upon his staff*, but it could equally be 'and Israel bowed himself upon the bed's head' (cf. Gn. xlvii. 29–31). The Vulgate renders this 'adored the top of his (Joseph's) staff'. Knox does not go as far as this, yet he translates 'made reverence to the top of Joseph's staff' and comments 'because the staff was a symbol of the tribe—cf. Numbers i. 49 where "the tribe of Levi" is literally "the staff of Levi"'. Cornelius a Lapide, however, suggested that through the ambiguous consonantal text the Holy Ghost intended both meanings, and he quoted this verse in defence of image-worship. It is quite impossible to accept the suggestion that the Holy Ghost intended both meanings, and it is equally impossible to find image-worship in such a quotation. Nairne rightly comments, 'If staves ever bore idolatrous images neither the LXX translations nor the writer of this Epistle were thinking of such antiquarian matters.' Its most probable meaning is that Jacob, being frail and weak, supported himself on his staff and bowed reverently before God. An excellent parallel is found in 1 Kings i. 47 where David bows himself in worship upon his bed in answer to a congratulatory blessing.

22. The commendation of Jacob's faith is now followed by that of Joseph who was firmly convinced that the promise given to Abraham would be fulfilled. At the end of his life, therefore, he gave commandment that at the Exodus his bones should be carried to the land of promise (cf. Gn. l. 24, 25). Joseph's request was honoured by Moses (Ex. xiii. 19) and fulfilled by Joshua (Jos. xxiv. 32).

23. The author now moves from Genesis to Exodus, from the age of the patriarchs to that of Moses, the leader of Israel, but he introduces the great lawgiver by first mentioning the faith of the parents who preserved his life as a babe. In the Hebrew of Exodus ii. 2 only the mother of Moses is mentioned as hiding the child, but the LXX, which is followed by our author, mentions both parents. In some way they saw in his beauty a promise of future blessing and believed that God had chosen him for some great purpose and would, therefore, preserve his life. Acts vii. 20 states that Moses was beautiful in the sight of God, *tō Theō*.

24, 25. *Moses, when he was come to years*, or 'when he was grown up', i.e. when he was fully forty years old (according to Acts vii. 23), faced one of the greatest crises of his life. He decided to break with the splendour of the Egyptian court and throw in his lot with the despised people of God, who were at that time an insignificant band of slaves and in abject misery. His prospects at court were brilliant for there lay before him the title and position of the son of Pharaoh's daughter; and if Jewish tradition is correct, he had great prospects of gaining the throne itself. By faith he believed that God, through him, would deliver the children of Israel from the bondage of Egypt (cf. Acts vii. 25), therefore he *refused to be called the son of Pharaoh's daughter*. By faith he perceived eternal realities and in consequence he refused *to enjoy* for a brief duration *the pleasures of sin*. Sin in this verse has the meaning of apostasy from God, which here is identified with the abandonment of the communion of the people of God.

26. *The reproach of Christ* could mean that Moses endured the reproach for Christ's sake. The Exodus was typical of, and a preparation for, the great redemption of Christ. The reproach that Moses endured, therefore, in furtherance of the Exodus in this case would be for Christ's sake. Another meaning is that Moses bore the same reproach at the hand of the Egyptians which Christ had to endure in the highest degree at the hands of the Jews, and which many of God's children are called upon to endure at the hands of unbelievers. There is a further suggestion which identifies Jehovah or Yahweh, who revealed Himself to Moses from the bush, with the second Person of the Trinity. Certainly 1 Corinthians x. 4 refers to Christ as the spiritual Rock which followed the children of Israel in the wilderness. Moreover, as Christ is at times spoken of as Head of the Church in all ages, He may be regarded, even before the incarnation, as being reproached Himself in the reproach of Moses. 'What the author means here', says Manson, 'is that the Christ, the pre-incarnate Son of God, was actually a participant in the events of the Exodus, and Moses when he made his great decision, *ipso facto* accepted and identified himself with the Christ's sufferings.' All these suggestions have real truth in them, and it is more than possible that the author had such things in mind; yet he may have meant nothing more than that Moses suffered the reproach, having the coming of Christ in view.

27. *By faith he forsook Egypt* can refer either to Moses' flight from Pharaoh unto the land of Midian, or to the Exodus. Against the latter are the following objections: (i) The Passover in the text follows Moses' departure (verse 28), so if this refers to the Exodus it would conflict with the chronological order followed by the author as he gives his examples of faith. (ii) *He forsook* is singular, suggesting that he went alone. (iii) According to Exodus xii. 31 Moses finally left Egypt at the command of Pharaoh and, therefore, *not fearing the wrath of the king* would be irrelevant. Against the former is the statement of Exodus ii. 14, 15 which suggests that the flight of Moses to Midian was caused by fear of Pharaoh, whereas here Moses *forsook Egypt, not fearing the wrath of the king.* These two statements are not irreconcilable, however, for it is highly probable that Moses *forsook Egypt* when (as he believed) he went to his brethren as God's messenger and deliverer. Acts vii. 23–25 suggests an invitation to rebellion, and our author states that this was done fearlessly, but the lack of faith in his brethren forced him to flee. Philo describes Moses' action at this period of his life as a settled policy. *He endured* by faith, i.e. persevered in his schemes of liberation through his long weary exile, *as seeing him who is invisible.* 'The courage to abandon work on which one's heart is set, and accept inaction cheerfully as the will of God, is of the rarest and highest kind, and can be created and sustained only by the clearest spiritual vision.'[1]

28. *Pistei* is better translated 'by faith', as in the previous verse, than *through faith.* For the use of the perfect *pepoiēken, kept,* see note on vii. 6 and also on verse 17 of this chapter. Moffatt cites the perfect here as 'another aoristic perfect', but this is very doubtful. This verb is frequently used in the LXX for holding or celebrating *the passover,* but it is more likely to mean here 'he has made', i.e. instituted, the passover which still continues in force today as a perpetual witness of the great deliverance. This Jewish festival, which was celebrated on the fourteenth day of the month Nisan, continued until the early hours of the fifteenth. It was followed by the feast of unleavened bread, which commenced on the fifteenth day and ended on the twenty-first.

It was by faith that the Israelites obeyed God's command to

[1] Peake, *The Century Bible.*

sprinkle the blood of the slain paschal lambs on the lintel and doorposts of their houses. It was this kind of faith which revealed them as God's people and placed them under His protection. Where there was no faith no blood was sprinkled and, in consequence, the judgment of God fell upon *the firstborn*.

29. *By faith they passed through the Red sea*, i.e. Moses and the Israelites. The emphasis is still upon the faith of Moses, though the connection of *by faith* with *they passed through* seems to include the faith of the people. The Exodus account of this incident shows much unbelief among the people, but there must have been faith of some kind for them to go forward into the sea at Moses' command. The Egyptians perished because their movement forward was an act of presumption rather than an act of faith. 'By a daring not unlike this', says Bengel, 'many rush into eternity. When two do the same thing, it is not the same thing.' The Israelites were acting according to God's will, the Egyptians were not.

30. Since the author looked upon the wanderings in the wilderness as an example of unbelief rather than of faith, of apostasy rather than of fidelity, no mention is made of them. The capture of Jericho may have been chosen because it was the first campaign in the promised land. No conquest here meant no rest in the remainder of the land. Seven priests, bearing seven trumpets, and followed by the ark of the covenant, marched in solemn procession around the city for seven days, preceded and followed by a silent army. On the seventh day the city was compassed about seven times. The whole campaign was an amazing example of faith in God's word and promise, and of patient endurance.

31. From very ancient times efforts have been made to soften the phrase *by faith the harlot Rahab perished not*. The Codex Sinaiticus with one or two others inserted *epilegomenē*, 'the so-called'. This was, as Zuntz rightly says, 'an effort to comply with the traditional tendency to whitewash the *harlot Rahab*', but the author of Hebrews did not adopt this tendency. Rahab was a Gentile woman and a harlot who had heard of the mighty works of the Israelites, and in true prophetic manner interpreted them as the acts of Jehovah and placed her faith in the omnipotence and supremacy of the God of Israel (Jos. ii). The position of Rahab among the faithful has been doubted because of her manner of life. Not only was she a prostitute, but she lied to the king of Jericho's messengers *when she had received the spies with peace*, and she betrayed her own country. But her prostitution took place before she believed and the other incidents took place during partial enlightenment (cf. verse 11). This despised heathen woman, who became united with the people of God and also an ancestress of the Messiah, points to the universality of the gospel.

32–34. *What shall I more say?* The use of the deliberative subjunctive may suggest that the Epistle to the Hebrews was originally a sermon, but as Robertson points out, 'it is both a literary and an oratorical idiom here'. The author finds in the history of Israel too many examples of overcoming and enduring faith for him to continue his description of them in detail. He supplies only a few names from the book of Judges and from the books of Samuel. The names are divided into pairs, but the order in each pair is strange, for the second in history becomes the first in the quotation. Among the judges *Gedeon* is mentioned first (though he came after Barak), probably as being the most famous hero, as well as being more remarkable in the history for faith and heroism. Israel's life under the judges is represented by *Gedeon* and *Barak, Samson* and *Jephthae*; under the monarchy by *David*, the greatest of Israel's kings, and under the prophetic order by *Samuel*.

The deeds enumerated in verses 33 and 34 need not be assigned exclusively to particular heroes, but may rather be taken as denoting generally the kind of exploits by which faith was evidenced throughout the history.

Who . . . subdued kingdoms is a general phrase covering the exploits of Gideon who smote the Midianites (Jdg. vii), of Barak who overcame the Canaanites (Jdg. iv), of Samson who slew the Philistines (Jdg. xiv. ff.), and of Jephthah who subdued the Ammonites (Jdg. xi). It is most unlikely that the phrase would exclude the great victories of David, the great conqueror of the Philistines (2 Sa. v. 17–28, viii. 1, xxi. 15 ff.), of the Moabites, Syrians and Edomites (2 Sa. viii. 2 ff.). *Wrought righteousness* is also a general phrase referring to those judges and kings whose administration was righteous and just. Who *obtained promises* can mean either 'who came into possession of the blessings which God had promised them', or 'who had received words of promise from God'.

The next statements are personal ones. Though *stopped the mouths of lions* may refer to Samson (Jdg. xiv. 6) and to David (1 Sa. xvii. 34 ff.), it most certainly refers to Daniel (Dn. vi. 22), for the author continues to quote from the book of Daniel with the next phrase *quenched the violence of fire*. This reference is to the three companions of Daniel—Shadrach, Meshach and Abed-nego (Dn. iii), and the incident is also referred to in 1 Maccabees ii. 59, which uses the original names of the three young men, Hananiah, Azariah and Mishael. The author no doubt knew the books of the Maccabees, and he may be referring to them in this passage; but there is no reason to believe that by his use of *escaped the edge of the sword* he was referring exclusively to Maccabees. This, like the others, is a general reference, for it can easily refer to David (1 Sa. xviii. 11, xix. 10, 12, xxi. 10), or to Elijah (1 Ki. xix. 1 ff.), or to Elisha (2 Ki. vi. 14 ff., 31 ff.). Even the words *out of weakness were made strong*, which could refer to the recovery in the days of the Maccabees, should be taken as a general reference including such incidents as the recovery of Hezekiah (2 Ki. xx; Is. xxxviii), the reinvigoration of the weakened Samson (Jdg. xvi. 28 ff.), and the strengthening of the whole people by restoration from the Babylonian captivity. The words *waxed valiant in fight, turned to flight the armies of the aliens* should be interpreted in the same manner, for although they may refer specially to the Maccabees they also fit the campaigns of Joshua, the Judges and David.

35. The first part of this verse refers to the raising from the dead of the son of the widow of Zarephath (1 Ki. xvii. 17 f.) and of the Shunammite woman by Elijah and Elisha respectively. These were raised to die again, but the second part of the verse refers to that *better resurrection*, i.e. a resurrection to eternal life. The reference to *others were tortured, etympanisthēzan,* is found in 2 Maccabees vi where it is recorded that Eleazar was 'tympanized', i.e. put on a rack and beaten to death in the time of Antiochus Epiphanes. Eleazar does not speak of the resurrection, but in 2 Maccabees vii, which records the death of a mother and her seven sons, three of the sons and their mother clearly proclaim their faith in the truth of the resurrection, not a mere resurrection to earthly life but to life everlasting.

36. The use of *heteroi, others,* introduces a particular class of heroes from among the *others* of the previous verse, but *mockings and scourgings* are frequently mentioned in 1 and 2 Maccabees, and the exceedingly severe and shameful tortures which came upon the seven brothers (2 Macc. vii. 1) are an excellent illustration of these words. Yet the author's purpose was to include another class of people who suffered severe tortures without suffering martyrdom as those did in verse 35. The mention of *bonds and imprisonment* reminds us of Joseph (Gn. xxxix. 20), Hanani (2 Ch. xvi. 10), Micaiah (1 Ki. xxii. 26, 27), Jeremiah (Je. xx. 2, xxxvii. 15).

37, 38. *They were stoned* may refer to Jeremiah of whom tradition stated that he was stoned to death in Egypt, but it is more probable that the author had Zechariah, son of Jehoiada, in mind (2 Ch. xxiv. 20, 21), an incident which was referred to by our Lord (see Mt. xxiii. 35–37). *Sawn asunder* denotes a mode of execution of which there is no instance either in the

Old Testament or Apocrypha; most probably it refers to a well-known Jewish tradition that Isaiah was sawn in two during the reign of Manasseh.

If *epeirasthēsan, were tempted,* is the correct reading then it seems an anticlimax after what has gone before. Its varying position in the MSS and its unsuitedness to the context led scholars as far back as Calvin and Erasmus to doubt its genuineness. It now seems in all probability to be a corrupt dittography of *epristhēsan, were sawn asunder,* for it is omitted by the Chester Beatty papyrus and two other minuscules. The RSV rightly omits the word.

Others *were slain with the sword,* such as Urijah who was murdered by Jehoiakim (Je. xxvi. 23). 1 Kings xix. 10 states: 'the children of Israel have . . . slain thy prophets with the sword.' There may also be a reference to the Jews who allowed themselves to be massacred on the sabbath at the commencement of the Maccabean wars (cf. 1 Macc. ii. 38).

A further picture of the sufferings of some of God's people is now given. (i) In regard to external habit, *they wandered about in sheepskins and goatskins.* Among those who wandered about in such clothing Elijah is perhaps the best known (2 Ki. i. 8). (ii) In regard to their personal condition, they were *destitute, afflicted, tormented* and accounted by the world as not worthy to live in it, whereas in fact they were of more value than the rest of mankind, and the world was an unworthy dwelling-place for them. (iii) In regard to their habitation, *they wandered in deserts, and in mountains, and in dens and caves of the earth,* like the hundred prophets hid by fifties by Obadiah in the days of Ahab and Jezebel (1 Ki. xviii. 4, 13), or like the Maccabeans, especially Judas and his men who were forced to take to the hills for safety (2 Macc. v. 7).

39, 40. *These all, having obtained a good report through,* i.e. in virtue of, *their faith,* witness was borne to them by God and the Scriptures. Yet, even so, they *received not the promise. These all* is not a reference to the *others* of verse 35 as some suggest, but to all the heroes of faith mentioned from verse 4 onwards. It is possible that *these* is an interpolation, for it is omitted by the Chester Beatty papyrus, Minuscule 1739, and by Clement and Augustine. The saints of the old covenant did not receive the promise behind all promises. They certainly saw the fulfilment of some promises, for Abraham received the promised son, but they did not receive the promise of the eternal inheritance. Lack of faith was not the reason, but the fact that God's purpose was not confined to those under the old covenant.

For *having provided* the RSV has 'foreseen', which, although a literal translation, does not give such a full meaning as the AV. Having foreseen, God makes provision. Until the revelation of redemption through the death and resurrection of Christ had taken place, no believers could ever attain to this eternal inheritance. God's purpose in history was wider than the Jewish nation, and His decree has gone forth that believers from that nation can never attain to the consummation until the number of the elect be accomplished, and all the redeemed of all ages shall be gathered together in one through Christ, and God shall be all in all.

c. The hope of the future promotes endurance in the present (xii. 1–29)

The readers, having such a great multitude of glorious examples of faith and a clear vision of Jesus, the divine originator of faith, are urged to endure the conflict (1–3). Their sufferings are to be regarded as a salutary chastisement on the part of God who is full of tender love and compassion towards them (4–13). Divine privileges have spiritual responsibilities within the Church (14–17). Reasons for the spiritual responsibilities are that the readers have been brought under the light of the gospel and into fellowship with God, the society of heaven and the Church on earth (18–24). The fifth and final warning concludes the section (25–29).

The spiritual race, xii. 1–3. The author now moves away from

188

the sphere in which the battle of faith must be fought, and pictures the Christian life as a race in which all Christians are competitors within the arena. The way of victory is exactly the same, however, as that of the saints in chapter xi who 'endured, as seeing him who is invisible'.

1. In the exhortation to run the race with patient endurance the author includes himself amongst the competitors. For their encouragement he points out that they are *compassed about with so great a cloud of witnesses* who, by their victorious lives, have borne personal testimony to the faith. Some commentators have pictured these Old Testament heroes as spectators of the race. The word 'witness' can mean 'spectator', but the context suggests that the runners are to look at *them* rather than they at the runners. Moreover, throughout the Epistle, and especially in chapter xi, 'witness' invariably means 'one who bears witness', i.e. one who testifies to a certain fact, and this is the more natural meaning here. In later times it came to mean one who is faithful unto death in his witness-bearing, a martyr. Nothing can be drawn from this passage as to the relation of the living and the dead.

It is next pointed out that though Christians have such a great multitude of glorious examples of enduring faith to encourage them, they must be ever watchful of obstructions which, unless removed, will certainly impede their progress. Those hindrances are first likened to 'weights' which must be *laid aside*. The Greek word *ogkon, weight*, in the athletic world of that day was connected with bulk of body or superfluous flesh which had to be removed by right training. It was also used metaphorically for pride, whether good or bad. But the use of the aorist, *apothemenoi, lay aside*, suggests something which can be thrown off like a garment, which in any race would be a great hindrance. *Ogkon* is used in a general sense suggesting that the Christian must throw off every hindrance in the race. *Euperistatos, easily beset*, can be either active or passive in force, a fact which has brought forth many interpretations apart from the one found in the AV. In the vernacular Greek, according to Deissmann, *peristasis* often means 'distress', 'evil circumstances', which gives support to Theophylact's interpretation 'because of which one easily falls into distresses'. Strangely enough the Chester Beatty papyrus has the reading *euperispastos*, 'so easily distracts', and Zuntz takes this to be the correct meaning. Some commentators have rendered the phrase 'the sin which men admire', but this seems out of harmony with the context. The RSV, and also Knox, translates 'clings so closely', and this is most probably the correct meaning. The sin which clings so closely cannot be the sin of apostasy itself, but it could be sin which leads to apostasy, such as the sin of nationalism which was clinging so closely to some of the readers who, failing to break from it, were still at the starting-post of the Christian life, but it may simply mean sin in general.

2. Having brought to their remembrance the many examples of patient endurance through vision of the unseen, the author now urges them to look away from external Judaism, to *Jesus the author and finisher of our faith. Our* is not found in the Greek but is added by both the AV and RV to elucidate *archēgos, author,* which Knox translates 'origin' and RSV 'pioneer'. The latter part of this Greek word presents little difficulty for it is obviously derived from '*agō*', 'to lead'; but the first part may be derived from either the active or middle of the verb *archō*. If it is derived from the active then the idea of 'supremacy' must be connected with the word, but if from the middle then the idea is one of 'source' or 'origin'. Even from the context it is not easy to decide whether Jesus is the supreme exemplar or the originator of faith. The author has given a long catalogue of heroes renowned for their faith as examples, and it is not unreasonable to deduce from this that he had in mind Jesus as the supreme exemplar of faith, for He endured the cross and despised its shame. Yet it is hardly possible that the author would assert that Christ's faith was similar to that of His followers. It seems better then to conceive of Christ as the originator of the Christian faith within the believer. In that case it is almost certain that *teleiōtēs*, most probably coined by the author himself, means 'completer', 'finisher'. In ii. 10 Jesus is the source and captain of our salvation, leading God's children to the heavenly promised land. The thought here is that He who begins a good work within the believer will certainly bring it to a triumphant issue.

Because of the joy which was to be a reward of His sufferings, Jesus *endured the cross*. In like manner the prospect of future blessedness should sustain believers under the strain and stress of the evils of this present time. The use of *anti, for*, by the author has led some to interpret the passage as if Jesus, instead of retaining that heavenly glory which He already had as the pre-incarnate logos, gave it up 'in order to accept and fulfil His redeeming office'. Manson is right when he says that such a conception is found in St. Paul, especially in Philippians ii. 5 ff., but not in this passage, for the joy appears to be a reward for what Christ endured in His own person on the cross. Calvin fancifully renders it, 'though it was free to Christ to exempt Himself from all trouble and to lead a happy life, abounding in all things, He yet underwent a death that was bitter and in every way ignominious.'

3. Both the cross and its cost have been discussed and now the readers are asked to reckon up the sufferings of Christ in order to compare them with their own, for such a comparison will preserve the soul from faintness and the steps from faltering. There cannot be any reasonable doubt that the overwhelming weight of MS evidence is in favour of the RV reading 'against themselves', yet according to Zuntz *against himself* is the only imaginable reading that fits the context. If 'against themselves' is correct, then it is explained by the words which are used in Numbers xvi. 38 of Korah, Dathan and Abiram who were their own worst enemies; they knew not what they did. In a similar manner those who sinned against Jesus were acting against their better selves and contrary to the promptings of their own hearts. If *against himself* is correct then the meaning is that Christ endured even those sinners who falsely denied His messianic claims and contended against His divine Sonship.

Verses 4–13 cover the subject of God's chastisement. The readers are reminded that though they have suffered severely, they have not been required to seal their faith by martyrdom (4). The chastisement of God is a sign of sonship, and there is always a divine purpose behind it (5–13).

4. The sufferings which the readers had been called upon to endure had not by any means reached the severity of Gethsemane or the cross; nor had these sufferings, severe though they were, resulted in martyrdom, as had happened in the experience of many Old Testament saints and of many of the Maccabeans. Some have maintained that the Epistle was written before there was any general martyrdom, therefore the reminder of a martyrdom not yet endured is remote from the context. All that the writer is saying is that the readers had not been in deadly earnest in their resistance of sin, and their half-heartedness had placed them in danger of apostasy. The former interpretation is certainly closer to the context.

5, 6. The AV translates this verse as an assertion *And ye have forgotten the exhortation,* but the context favours the interrogative 'And have ye forgotten the exhortation . . . ?' Chapter xiii. 22 describes the Epistle as a 'word of exhortation', which shows that one of the main purposes of the writer was to comfort and encourage his readers. Proverbs iii. 11, 12 is then used to bring out the Father's love for His children, rather than the example of Christ, who learned obedience by the things which He suffered. Christ's sufferings were not in the true sense either disciplinary or a punishment. The AV rightly translates *dialegetai, speaketh.* The Greek word frequently means 'reasoneth', and many take it to have this meaning here; yet unless the quotation of Proverbs is taken as a reply to the complaints of the readers this can hardly be the meaning. It is the author who is dealing with the complaints and he quotes Scripture as the voice of God speaking to them.

Paideias, chastening, in classical Greek means 'instruction', 'education', but in biblical Greek the instruction and education are given by means of correction through the severe discipline of God. The aim of such discipline remains the same but its use varies, for it is put in operation to deliver from sin, to perfect in holiness, or to establish in the faith; here it is administered to promote endurance. The readers are urged, therefore, not to despise or regard lightly such discipline as if God were not behind it, or to drift into despondency, for God never tries anyone beyond his strength. *Elegchomenos, art rebuked,* or 'reproved', suggests that by such reproof a person will be brought to acknowledge his fault (cf. Mt. xviii. 15). God's strong affection for the children *whom he receiveth,* or 'adopts', does not overrule His purpose for them, which is spiritual development to a fuller life of righteousness. He cannot, therefore, overlook those faults or misdemeanours which mar their spiritual growth.

7. There is a difficulty which makes *if ye endure chastening* a doubtful translation. The opening word *ei, if,* is not found in the best MSS which have *eis,* 'for', in its place. Some take *hupomenete, endure,* to be imperative and translate 'endure ye for chastening', i.e. regard and bear your trials as part of the moral training which God has purposed for you. It is more likely, however, to be indicative and rendered as the RV, 'It is for chastening that ye endure', i.e. the trials that come upon you are for your training; they are sent not in anger but in fatherly love, *for what son is he whom the father chasteneth not?* (cf. Dt. viii. 5; 2 Sa. vii. 14; Pr. xiii. 24).

8. The author cannot conceive of sonship without chastisement. Those who are without chastisement and claim to be sons are making a false claim. *Nothoi, bastards,* is found in Wisdom iv. 3 where it could mean 'spurious' or 'children who were born of the hated mixed marriages'; here, however, it means 'born out of wedlock', symbolizing those who, by rejecting God's discipline, prove themselves to be illegitimate, i.e. not true sons of God.

9. The discipline imposed upon the readers had brought discouragement and some had become disheartened. The author now argues that *fathers of our flesh*, or 'earthly fathers', disciplined their children and the children *gave them reverence.* Should not the children of God give similar respect to *the Father of spirits* whose divine purpose is always for their highest good? This strange phrase, the *Father of spirits*, does not mean the creator of angels and spirits, nor does it designate God as the Creator of souls; in fact it should not be used at all as a possible solution to later theological problems such as creationism (i.e. that God separately creates the soul of each one of us) and traducianism (i.e. that our souls are derived through our parents by hereditary descent from Adam). The phrase is simply used to bring out in vivid contrast the authors of men's physical existence to whom submission is given under discipline and the Author of spiritual beings to whom greater submission should be given, for not merely physical life but spiritual and eternal life come from Him.

10. Furthermore, the discipline of earthly fathers was *for a few days* (RSV, 'a short time'). The *few days* can hardly refer to the period of earthly life in comparison with eternity, for *we have had, eichomen* (verse 9) suggests that the discipline imposed upon the readers had come to an end when they had reached maturity. It must then refer to that period of childhood when the child is under the discipline of the father, which is of short duration. This brief authority of earthly fathers was displayed *after their own pleasure*, or 'according to their own judgment', which was at times capricious. This is vastly different from

God's discipline which is always *for our profit,* i.e. for the good of our spiritual welfare, enabling us to be more free from the power of sin and to become *partakers of his holiness.*

11. Use is now made of a general statement that discipline when it is imposed, whether it be human or divine, does not appear *to be joyous but grievous.* Yet when the author brings out the result, he has in mind only divine discipline. *The peaceable fruit of righteousness* has been taken as a genitive of origin, the peaceful fruit such as righteousness produces, but this is doubtful for the context makes it clear that it is discipline which produces fruit and that fruit is righteousness. It should, therefore, be taken as a genitive of apposition, the fruit which consists of righteousness. *Peaceable, eirēnikon,* is possibly used as Moffatt suggests in contrast to the restiveness and pain of the period of the discipline, when people are being trained.

12, 13. *Wherefore* brings the argument to a conclusion. Seeing that the discipline, which has brought discouragement because of its severity, has a gracious and beneficial purpose *lift up the hands which hang down, and the feeble knees.* The form of this exhortation agrees closely with Isaiah xxxv. 3 and Ecclesiasticus xxv. 23. The suggestion that there is a return once again to the metaphors of the fight and race is doubtful. Such metaphors as are used here were in common use to express slackness, faint-heartedness and mental flagging where the formal conception of a race is not present. This exhortation is addressed to the whole community to encourage them to be strong so that their loyalty and endurance may become an inspiring example to their weaker brethren in the faith. Thus they are urged to *make straight paths for* their *feet,* i.e. to go forward in the Christian path of life which had already been prepared for them by Christ Himself (x. 20). They were not to lean towards Judaism or even to mix Judaism with Christianity *lest that which is lame be turned out of the way. To chōlon, lame,* is a figurative description of the wavering between two different forms of belief. Westcott rightly suggests that 'the halting of the Hebrews' between two opinions 'is the characteristic type of their weakness' (1 Ki. xviii. 21). If the Christian community fails to have this settled form of belief then it will be unable to help him who makes only a staggering and wavering progress in the Christian faith. If, however, the community as a whole advances in a straight path, planned out for it by divine revelation in Scripture, then the tottering Christian will *be healed* of his defect by this stimulating example, and he will briskly advance with them.

14. The readers are now urged to *follow peace with all men* or 'strive for peace with all men' (rsv) or 'strive for peace with all Christians', which is better. Many commentators take this charge to be general and maintain that the readers were to seek peace even with non-Christians. This meaning of the phrase is equivalent to: 'If possible, so far as it depends upon you, live peaceably with all' (Rom. xii. 18, rsv). Moffatt places *meta* after *diōketē* and translates 'along with all the (other) Christians'. He suggests that the call is to make common cause with all the rest of the Christians in the quest for God's peace, i.e. 'the bliss and severity of a life under God's control'. Moffatt is right in confining *pantōn* to all other Christians, but the context gives little support to the idea of all Christians uniting together in striving after God's peace. Surely the author's object is to create harmony within the local community so that internal dissension, or separatist tendencies, may be put away, for a divided church is a real hindrance to the advancement of Christ's cause. There must be loyalty to the whole Christian Church but not at *any* cost, for their supreme aim must be devotedness to God, which alone produces purity of heart and life, and *without which no man shall see the Lord*. This exhortation to peace and purity within the Church suggests that Matthew v. 8, 9 was in mind and, if so, then *Lord* most certainly refers to God the Father. Yet, as Westcott points out, it may mean 'Christ for whose return in glory believers wait' (cf. ix. 28). The difficulty here, however, is the limitation of this vision to that definite revelation of God which is the result of Christ's second advent, whereas it may also mean an emblematic representation of an innermost vision through intimate personal fellowship with God.

15. True devotedness to Christ by any Christian community must bring harmony and holiness, yet unless that community takes heed of the actions of its individual members both may be destroyed. It must see, therefore, that each one is true to his Christian profession, for it is possible for a man to *fail of the grace of God*. *Husterōn, fail,* may have the same meaning as in iv. 1, but the use of *apo* after it may suggest a falling back from the grace of God. If the former is correct then the meaning would be that there was in the Christian community someone who was making a Christian profession but who had come short of the grace of God. If the latter is correct then it can only mean that there was someone within the community who had ceased to draw from the divine source of strength. Whichever meaning is correct the result on the spiritual life of the community is the same, for any unworthy member may be like a poisonous weed which has a devastating effect on everything round about it. *Rhiza pikrias, root of bitterness,* is a quotation from Deuteronomy xxix. 18, 'a root that beareth gall and wormwood' or, as in the margin, which is most probably the correct reading, 'a poisonous herb'.

16. The Church must also take heed to any indulgence in sensual sins, and to those who care more for the gains and worldly pleasures of this life than for the eternal realities of the unseen world. Of these latter persons *Esau* is given as an example. Although Jewish tradition describes him as a man of impure life, *pornos, fornicator,* may not refer to Esau in this text. Nowhere in Scripture is he referred to as a fornicator; but he is mentioned as a profane person who sold his spiritual inheritance *for one morsel of meat* or 'for a single meal' (RSV).

Manson is right when he affirms that 'it was unbelief in the divine promise to his house, not mere sensuality, that led Esau to the irrevocable step of bartering away his birthright. No later repentance was able to undo this act.'

17. The fatal result of Esau's behaviour, which was familiar to the Jewish readers, is now set forth as a warning. The blessing was appointed to the firstborn as the bearer of the promises given by God to Abraham and his seed. The birthright, therefore, was Esau's but this he rejected for a trivial material gain, thus showing that the blessing had no value in his sight. Afterwards when he was eager to gain possession of the blessing, *he was rejected* by God.

There is no record in the Old Testament of any repentance on the part of Esau. Genesis xxvii. 34 mentions that 'he cried with a great and exceeding bitter cry' when he realized that the blessing which he had bartered for a mess of pottage was finally lost. Some commentators suggest that *he found no place of repentance* refers to the unsuccessful efforts of Esau to change his father's mind. The blessing bestowed upon Jacob was not recalled. In this case one would have expected some such addition as *tou patros*, 'his father'. Others have placed the words in brackets as a parenthesis and have connected *autēn*, *it*, with *blessing* and not with *repentance*. According to this what Esau sought with tears was the blessing. *Ekzēteo* suggests that the seeker finds, or exhausts his powers in seeking. Here Esau had exhausted his powers in seeking a repentance which would undo the consequences of his former folly; but in this particular case there was no opportunity given for such repentance. The writer may have had in mind an idiom of Roman law whereby an opportunity was given to reconsider one's decision. The decision which Esau desired to be reconsidered was the selling of his birthright but no opportunity was given.

The Epistle now reaches a climax in a passage both graceful and ingenious (verses 18–24), in which is seen the surpassing attractiveness and supremacy of the new covenant as compared with the old. The author's aim in this is to show that higher privileges carry with them greater responsibilities.

18. The introductory *for* brings out the connection between the sanctification of God's people under the new covenant already mentioned in verse 14 and the sanctification of the people of Israel before they could even draw near to receive the law (Ex. xix. 10). No mention is made of Mount Sinai in the text, and *mount* is omitted by the best MSS, but the context makes it clear that the *mount that might be touched* is Mount Sinai. *Psēlaphōmenō, that might be touched,* is not the same Greek word as that which is used in verse 20, and its meaning here is most probably 'tangible'. E. C. Selwyn has suggested a conjectural reading *pephopsalōmenō*, which he translates 'a calcined volcano'. The word 'tangible' implies that the terrifying manifestations of burning fire, whirlwind, darkness and storm through which God revealed Himself to the Israelites were felt by the senses. The readers when they became Christians had no experiences of any such visible and repellent phenomena. What they experienced was entirely spiritual and gracious.

19, 20. The language here is reminiscent of Deuteronomy iv. 12 'And the Lord spake unto you out of the midst of the fire', of Exodus xix. 16 'the voice of the trumpet', and of Exodus xix. 19 'God answered him by a voice'. The voice, which according to Westcott 'was most intelligible, most human and articulate', seems to have filled the Israelites with terror so that they *intreated that the word should not be spoken to them any more* except through the mediator Moses (Ex. xx. 19). According to Deuteronomy v. 23 f. the leaders of the nation, through fear of the voice and the fire, appealed to Moses to be their mediator before God and to bring His messages to them.

The author, using an abbreviated form of Exodus xix. 12, 13, states that *they could not endure* the command, *and if so much as a beast touch the mountain, it shall be stoned.* The words *thrust through with a dart* are absent from the ancient MSS, and were added to complete the quotation from Exodus xix. 13 LXX.

21. An unnecessary difficulty has been raised about the expression *I exceedingly fear and quake* ascribed by the author to Moses, because it does not appear in the accounts of the promulgation of the law given in the Pentateuch. 'I exceedingly fear' is found in Deuteronomy ix. 19 LXX, though there is no mention there of *and quake*; and these words describe Moses' sense of God's wrath at the time of the worshipping of the golden calf, which took place after the giving of the law. The words 'Moses trembled' are also found in Acts vii. 32 where they refer to the incident of the 'burning bush' (Ex. iii); but they are not found in the Pentateuch. There is no need to suggest, however, as Owen does, that this knowledge came to the author from immediate inspiration! Others have connected the present verse with Exodus xix. 16, 17 and, possibly, 19, where it is recorded that *all* the people trembled, concluding that Moses was among them. It has been further suggested, quite reasonably, that the author may, almost unconsciously, have compressed into one the incident of the 'burning bush' (Ex. iii) and the apostasy of Israel in the worship of the golden calf (Dt. ix. 19). But as Moses' terror is frequently mentioned in Jewish writers, and as the author occasionally makes use of well-known Jewish traditions, he may, like Stephen in Acts vii. 32, have made use of one here, which does not in any way deny the truth of the fact asserted by the inspired writer.

22. Under the old covenant Israel was God's own chosen religious community. *Mount Sion* was the place of worship, and *Jerusalem* was looked upon as the place of His presence. A description is now given of a wider communion into which the readers have entered through acceptance of the Christian faith. *Proseléluthate, ye are come*, or 'ye have come', being in the perfect, does not refer to some communion into which believers enter after death but to a communion into which they enter when Christianity is embraced. Those who have this experience have already come to the celestial order, to the spiritual *mount Sion . . . the city of the living God, the heavenly Jerusalem* in contrast to the material Mount Sinai. Believers have not come to terrible manifestations but into God's presence, to the very throne of grace, through their mediator Jesus Christ. They have also come *to an innumerable company of angels*, i.e. into God's court consisting of 'myriads' or 'tens of thousands' of angels (cf. Dt. xxxiii. 2; Ps. lxviii. 17; Dn. vii. 10).

23. E. F. Moulton and others do not limit *general assembly* to the angels but regard it as descriptive also of the *church of the firstborn*, but the following expression *which are written in heaven* does not support this suggestion. The same objection must be made to the theory which identifies the *church of the firstborn* with the heroes of the past who valued their birthright, in contrast to Esau who despised his. The phrase has also been interpreted as the Church triumphant and the Church universal, but the words *which are written in heaven* strongly suggest that the believers referred to are still on earth and that they have been enrolled in the heavenly register (cf. Lk. x. 20; Rom. viii. 16, 29; Jas. i. 18). This is also supported by the expression *the spirits of just men made perfect*. When a man believes, he has no dreadful experiences to undergo like the Israelites, but has immediate access into God's presence, and becomes an inhabitant of the heavenly city, which consists of myriads of angels, of the saints on earth, and of *the spirits of just men made perfect*, i.e. of the faithful departed, including the saints of both covenants, who have already been led by the Captain of their salvation to the higher state of blessedness.

It is an obvious fact that God is *the Judge of all*; but from the order of the Greek words a more correct translation would be 'have come to Him as Judge, who is God over all'. This supreme God, Sovereign over all nations and people, is also

Judge; to Him the readers have come, and far from finding condemnation, they have found grace and fellowship.

24. The reason is now given why the readers were not consumed by God's judgment. They have come to *Jesus the mediator of the new covenant* who stands between the Holy God and the guilty sinner. This *covenant*, unlike the one which, because of its ineffectiveness, had grown old, is *new* both in the time of its appearance and in its quality. It was established through *the blood of sprinkling*, i.e. through Jesus' atoning blood which has been accepted by God and sprinkled upon the hearts of all believers. Because of its effectiveness in bringing reconciliation, forgiveness and spiritual power, it *speaketh better things than that of Abel*, for Abel's blood, according to Jewish tradition, cried only for vengeance.

A final warning in verses 25–29 brings to a conclusion the writer's argument that greater privileges carry with them greater responsibilities. If the Israelites with a partial and limited revelation became liable to God's judgment because of disobedience, an incomparably severer punishment would fall upon the readers who rejected this new revelation of God and its accompanying blessings.

25. The readers are urged to beware lest they *refuse . . . him that speaketh*, i.e. God, to whom reference is also made in the phrase *him that spake on earth*. The comparison is not between the two mediators, Moses and Christ, but between the two revelations, the old and the new. The AV, by using the words *speaketh* and *spake* for two different Greek words, does not do justice to the different meanings conveyed by them. *Lalounta, speaketh*, is also used in i. 1 and has the same meaning, whereas *chrēmatizonta, spake*, has a similar meaning to that found in viii. 5. RSV rightly translates 'warned'. *Paraitēsamenoi, refused*, is in verse 19 translated 'intreated'. The Israelites entreated or begged that no further communication be given them except through Moses, and their action was commended by God (Dt. v. 28). 'Their sin', says Westcott, 'was not in the request that Moses only should speak to them (Deut. v. 28), but in the temper which made the request necessary.' The Israelites did not escape the consequences of their persistent rejection of the revelation of God given through Moses.

26–28. Two quotations are now brought forward and compared with each other to show the superiority of the new revelation over the old. The first, which speaks of the *voice* which *then shook the earth*, is drawn from Exodus xix. 18 f., but the author, contrary to his normal custom, does not follow the LXX which substitutes 'the amazement of the people' for 'the shaking of the people'. The second, which refers not to a voice but to God who promised to shake both earth and heaven, is from Haggai ii. 6, and the prophecy was taken to imply that a new and heavenly order would arise over the ruins of the old. In a similar way, after the final shaking of the whole creation and the passing away of the visible earth and heavens, God's heavenly city and eternal *kingdom*, in which all Christians have a part, will remain unshaken. The visible earth and heavens, which are removed, are only shadows of the heavenly and eternal, just as the Jewish polity, which is also removed, is only a shadow of the Christian dispensation. Yet, as Westcott rightly reminds us, 'The "invisible" archetypes are also, as all things, "made" by God (Isa. lxvi. 22)'. They are not imperishable in themselves but they abide in virtue of the divine will, which they, being spiritual, are peculiarly fitted to express. Therefore, the author concludes, in the light of the permanency, stability and superiority of Christianity, *let us have grace*. This may refer to the Christian drawing near to the throne of grace to find grace to help in time of need (cf. iv. 16), but the balance of argument seems in favour of the meaning 'Therefore let us be grateful' (RSV). A thankful recognition of the higher privileges, which have been bestowed upon Christians, is a certain remedy for discouragement, which is displeasing to God, and a strong encouragement to the worshipper to offer with reverent fear and awe a service well-pleasing to Him.

29. The reason why God must be approached with reverent fear and awe lies in the fact that there is another aspect of His character besides that of grace. *Our God is a consuming fire.* Some commentators have translated 'for our God too is a consuming fire', which suggests that the God of the Christians, like the God of the old covenant, *is a consuming fire.* Apart from the fact that in this case one would have expected *our* to have been placed before *God* and not afterwards, constant expression is given throughout the Epistle to the writer's belief that the God of the old covenant is also the God of the new. A further and deeper reason why this aspect of God's character, so frequently found in the Old Testament (cf. Ex. xxiv. 17; Dt. v. 4; Is. xxxiii. 14), is stressed is to warn the readers against a false acceptance of the Christian faith. At the second advent of Jesus Christ, just as the material and transitory will disappear and the eternal and permanent will remain, so what is false and vile will be revealed in the fire of God's holiness and those whose characters are such will be consumed by the fire of His judgment.

VIII. FINAL PRACTICAL EXHORTATIONS
(xiii. 1–25)

The concluding exhortations deal first with the individual Christian's duties towards other Christians (1–6), and then with his special duties within the Church's fellowship, among which are submission to pastoral and to spiritual authority, and most important of all, complete devotion to his Lord and Master Jesus Christ (7–17). The Epistle ends with personal references and affectionate greetings (18–25).

a. Practical Christian duties (xiii. 1–6)

The author specifies two ways in which the duty of love must be given practical expression (1–3). He then exhorts his readers to purity of life (4) and to contentment (5), at the same time warning them against the adulterers and covetous.

1. Not only was *brotherly love* a new and hitherto almost un-dreamed-of virtue, but it was particularly necessary among the members of a bitterly persecuted sect. According to vi. 10 and x. 33, 34, the readers had already exercised this virtue and were still exercising it. Yet the action of some readers in neglecting the assembly for Christian worship and fellowship revealed a danger of the Christian bond of love being severed, and so the exhortation to continue was of special importance.

2, 3. The author signifies two modes by which it is essential that brotherly love should be manifested. The first, hospitality, was not to be confined to those Christians who were known to the readers, but to be extended to Christian brethren from other lands or districts. Owing to the hatred of the Jews for the Christians it was extremely difficult for those Christians, who were travelling on business or in the service of the Church, or had been driven from their homes through persecution, to find accommodation. Encouragement to entertain is given in the words *some have entertained angels unawares. Some*, although not necessarily confined to Abraham and Lot, specially refers to them (cf. Gn. xviii, xix). It is not necessary to suppose that the author was suggesting that, in entertaining the Christian brethren, they might be entertaining some supernatural beings; the thought is rather that among the brethren there might be true messengers of God. Yet he may have had in mind the declaration of our Lord that whoever entertains one of His servants entertains the Lord Himself (Mt. xxv. 44, 45).

The second expression of sympathy was also of a practical nature. They were to *remember*, i.e. bear in mind, those who were in bonds, in order to aid them with ministering love. Their practical sympathy was to be exercised with as much devotion as if they themselves were also prisoners. *Hōs sundedemenoi, as bound with them*, could mean that they themselves were prisoners, but it is doubtful whether the phrase has such a meaning here. The thought is similar to that found in 1 Corinthians xii. 26, RSV: 'If one member suffers, all suffer together.' Yet this does not imply that *as being yourselves also in the body* refers to their membership in the body of Christ, the Church, as Calvin suggests. *The body* here is the earthly body, and while they sojourn in such a body, the readers themselves are liable to similar treatment.

4. The author now seeks to promote marriage to its rightful place as a divine ordinance. As there is no verb in the Greek, the AV supplies *estin* and translates *marriage is honourable in all*; but as the following phrase, *and the bed undefiled,* must be an exhortation, it is better to supply *estō* and, to render the words as in RSV, 'Let marriage be held in honour . . . and let the marriage bed be undefiled'. *En pasin, in all,* may be neuter or masculine. If it is masculine, it may mean that marriage should be highly esteemed by all who are married and not desecrated by adultery, or that it should be held in high estimation by married and unmarried alike. Calvin and many others maintain that it is directed against false asceticism (1 Tim. iv. 3), and that marriage should be denied to no order or class of men. If *en pasin* is neuter, the exhortation is not limited to chastity but extends to the whole of married life. In all respects the readers are urged to hold marriage in high estimation. The second half of this exhortation is added to encourage purity in physical intimacy. It is a plain warning against any violation of the marriage bond. Those who lightly regard this bond may escape the judgment of men, yet if unrepentant, they will never escape God's judgment.

5, 6. In the New Testament the usual Greek word for *conversation,* or 'manner of life', is *anastrophē*; but the Greek word used in this passage is *tropos*, which can mean 'manner of life', or 'the way of thought and life'. The Christian's habits of thought and life in connection with money are a touchstone of his character. Such habits must be free from covetousness and avarice, for the love of money can be as detrimental to a man's spiritual life as sensuality. The way of victory over this evil is to *be content with such things as ye have*. This high Christian standard of contentment would be beyond the reach of most believers but for the promise of God's presence and protection. Paul could say, 'I have learned, in whatsoever state I am, therewith to be content,' because he could also say 'I can do all things through Christ, which strengtheneth me' (Phil. iv. 11–13).

Although the exact words, *for he hath said, I will never leave thee, nor forsake thee*, do not occur in the Old Testament, the same meaning is frequently found (cf. Gn. xxviii. 15; Dt. xxxi. 6; Jos. i. 5; Is. xli. 17). The encouragement lies in the fact that it is God Himself who gives us the blessed assurance of His presence and help. With such assurance in our hearts *we may boldly say, The Lord is my helper, and I will not fear what man shall do unto me*. The last clause *what man shall do unto me* is better taken as an independent direct question 'what can man do to me?' (so RSV). The best commentary on this quotation from Psalm cxviii. 6 is 'If God be for us, who can be against us?' (Rom. viii. 31).

b. Necessary religious duties (xiii. 7–17)

An exhortation is given to the readers to remember former leaders and to imitate their faith (7, 8). They must also eschew unchristian doctrines and purely external religious observances (9–17).

7. The author now moves away from exhortation bearing upon the individual's practical Christian life to that which affects his church relations and religious beliefs. The first exhortation is to *remember them which have the rule over you*, or 'remember your leaders' (RSV). In verses 17 and 24 the reference is to the leaders who were living, but here it is to those spiritual leaders who had finished the course and kept the faith. These leaders are without doubt those immediate disciples of the Lord mentioned in ii. 3 from whom they had received the Word of God. *Ekbasis, end,* may refer to the results of the holy lives which those early leaders lived while they preached the Word of God; but the context suggests that it is used here, as in Wisdom ii. 17, as a metaphor for death, though not necessarily a death by martyrdom. However, the fact that the readers are earnestly to contemplate the end of these men's lives suggests that there was something extraordinary about their death. Moffatt thinks that their death was remarkable for its witness to faith. He therefore concludes that they had laid down their lives as martyrs. By the contemplation of these leaders in life and death the readers will be strengthened to imitate their faith.

8. This verse is a connecting link between what precedes and what follows. Whether in life or in death the leaders bore testimony to the unchangeableness of Christ. This fact was the ground of their consistent loyalty to the Christian faith and the inspiration of their lives. They have passed away, but their Lord and Saviour not only abides for ever but remains the same—the eternal, unchangeable Christ. The readers, having the same ground for consistency and the same inspiring power, must not waver nor allow any doctrines opposed to the doctrines which have been taught them to find a place in their thoughts.

9. Jesus Christ is God's last unchangeable message to His people, never to be superseded or supplemented. It seems evident that the form of error arising within the community to which the Epistle is addressed challenged the supremacy and unchangeableness of Christ. It is difficult to say what these *divers* (RSV, 'diverse') *and strange doctrines* were. The only clue comes from the mention of *brōmata, meats,* which reminds us of similar warnings in St. Paul's Epistles (cf. Rom. xiv. 2, 14, 21; Col. ii. 8, 16–23, etc.). These 'teachings' were being given by those who were serving the tabernacle, and who were insisting that external ordinances were necessary for salvation rather than a reliance solely on God's grace. These outward ordinances had not profited the Jews in the past, and there was no reason to believe that they would benefit Christians now or in the future.

10. The author now emphasizes that *we*, i.e. we Christians, *have an altar* from which those who serve the tabernacle have no right to eat. The altar is the place of sacrifice and not the sacrifice itself. In the old covenant the place of sacrifice was the brazen altar. There the sin offering was made. The Jewish people, who acknowledged this form of religion and were partakers of its ritual on atonement day, had no right to be partakers of the Christian altar or the Christian place of sacrifice, i.e. the cross, which was the antitype of the brazen altar. Upon this altar the body of Christ was offered once for all, and the all-sufficiency of the sacrifice has been frequently shown in this Epistle. To acknowledge any other place of sacrifice is to deny the all-sufficiency of Christ's sacrifice.[1]

11, 12. The atoning sacrifice represented by *those beasts* which were offered on the brazen altar and *whose blood* was *brought into the sanctuary* typically prefigured the one great atoning sacrifice of Christ. Neither the high priest nor anyone else under the old covenant was permitted to eat of the bodies of these sin-offerings which were *burned without* (i.e. outside) *the camp*. Although they were partakers of the benefits of the offerings sacrificed upon the Jewish altar, they did not literally partake of the flesh of these sacrificial victims. So also Christians, although partakers of the benefits of Christ's work on the cross, cannot literally partake of Christ's body. 'In real Christian worship', as Moffatt says, 'there is no sacrificial meal; the great sacrifice is not one of which the worshippers partake by eating.'

[1] See further, Additional Note, p. 211.

13. To fulfil the type it was not necessary for Christ to suffer outside the camp, or beyond the gate of the holy city. The fact that He did so signified that He had been cast out by those under the old covenant. The exhortation *let us go forth therefore unto him* means that no longer must the readers look for salvation in the old forms of Judaism; they must come outside of it to Jesus who cannot be found in Judaism. They must bear His reproach (rsv 'abuse for Him') by coming to His cross of shame, which was an object of disgust to the Gentiles, and to the Jews the place of a curse, since they regarded every crucified person as 'accursed of God' (Dt. xxi. 22, 23; Gal. iii. 13). And they must then be prepared to bear the reproach of Christ even if it should lead to excommunication or martyrdom.

14. The reason is now stated why they should be willing to bear this reproach; *for here,* i.e. upon earth, they *have no continuing city, but . . . seek one to come.* Like the great cloud of witnesses already mentioned in chapter xi, on this earth they are strangers and pilgrims looking to 'the city which is to be', 'the city which hath foundations'.

15. The author now comes to his closing exhortation and urges the readers to offer to God through Christ the spiritual sacrifices of praise and thanksgiving. Great emphasis is placed upon *di'autou, by him,* for their sacrifices of praise and thanksgiving must be offered not through the intervention of the Jewish sacrificial order, or any other order, but through Christ the one great High Priest and Mediator of the new covenant. The *sacrifice of praise,* which is to be offered *continually,* is in opposition to the animal sacrifices which have ceased, and implies that the one perfect sacrifice has already been offered and accepted by God.

16. The offering of the heart to God in praise and thanksgiving must be followed by the sacrifice of love manifested in good deeds and in a free sharing of possessions. Moffatt rightly points out that the three great definitions of worship or religious service in the New Testament (here, and in Rom. xii. 1 f. and Jas. i. 27) are all inward and ethical.

17. In verse 7 the readers were exhorted to remember those spiritual leaders who had passed on, and especially their consistency in life and doctrine. They are now urged to obey those spiritual leaders who were still in their midst, and to submit themselves to their authority, for in them the same consistency in life and doctrine is found. The repetition of the injunction about the spiritual leaders may indicate a tendency to self-assertion and spurious independence amongst themselves. Christians must always retain the liberty wherewith Christ has made them free; but insubordination to the spiritual leaders chosen by God can mar the spiritual welfare and progress of the Church. Bengel tersely differentiates between obedience and submission when he says, 'obey in those things which they command you to do as salutary: submit even when they demand a little more'. The author proceeds to give some reasons and motives for this spiritual obedience and submission. The leaders have the solemn responsibility of keeping watch over their souls with a view to their salvation, and of rendering an account of their conduct in this matter to God at the appearing of Jesus Christ. Readiness to obey and submit would encourage the leaders to do their responsible work *with joy, and not with grief.* Their grief is not the result of any failure or imperfection in their work, but is due to the self-will and resentment under discipline of the readers. Such grief in the hearts of the leaders will mean spiritual loss for those to whom the Epistle was addressed.

Additional note on xiii. 10

This verse has evoked many theories, and at the moment no one theory holds the field. A few commentators, mostly conservative, maintain that the author was referring to a Jewish altar. This theory is built upon the claim that the Epistle was written to Hebrews and, therefore, the passage refers to them and to the Old Testament. They assert that the 'we' implied in *echomen, we have*, is not 'we Christians' but 'we Hebrews'. *Echomen*, on this theory, does not mean 'we have now', i.e. at the moment of writing the Epistle; but 'as Moses delivered it to us in the ceremonial law'. *They . . . which serve the tabernacle* from this point of view means the Levitical priests. The *altar* is Jewish, and it must refer to the altar of sin-offering in Leviticus xvi, and is used by metonymy for the sacrifice connected with the altar. The difficulty of this theory lies in the fact that, although the writer is most probably a Jew, he seems to be writing as a Christian to Hebrews who had also made a confession of Christianity.

Most commentators, therefore, assert that the author is speaking of a Christian altar. *We* (Christians) *have an altar*: but there is a diversity of opinion about the interpretation of *altar*. Some, including Calvin and Owen, make Christ the altar, but there is a harshness in the suggestion which makes Christ at one and the same time the altar, sacrifice and priest.

Peake put forward the view that the altar on the day of atonement was really the mercy-seat; so the Christian altar would be in the heavenly sanctuary where the blood was applied. But there is no suggestion that the word 'altar' was used for the mercy-seat either in the Old Testament or in this Epistle. Nor does the author conceive of Christ applying His blood on an altar in the heavenly sanctuary. Leonard rightly says, 'it is clear that any local sprinkling of blood within the heavenly tabernacle is, even in a metaphorical sense, unthinkable.' An ancient theory suggests that the author is underlining the difference between the Christian sacrifice and the Jewish. Christians have a right to eat of their altar, but the Jews have not. This implies that Christian believers partake of a sacrificial feast and, therefore, the author had in mind the Christian Eucharist. Westcott made the following paraphrase: 'We Christians have an altar, from which we draw the material for our feast. . . . Our privilege is greater than that of the priest or high-priest under the Levitical system. Our great sin-offering . . . is given to us as food. . . .'

The context, however, does not give the slightest hint that the Christian Eucharist was in the mind of the author. Indeed it suggests that the Christians have no sacrificial food to eat, and, previous to verse 10, there is a negative attitude taken towards foods. According to Peake, the author is saying: 'Because Jesus is the supreme sin-offering, it is impossible that His body should be eaten in a sacrificial meal.' Moffatt also argues in a similar way, 'His point', he says, 'is simply this, that the Christian sacrifice, on which our relationship to God depends, is not one that involves or allows any connexion with a meal.' He goes further and argues that the author is opposing a neo-sacramentalism which conceived the Lord's Supper as an eating of the body of Christ.

Creed sees very little reason to hold that beliefs with regard to the Eucharist were of controversial interest in the first century, and maintains that, had this been the case, the writer would not have expressed himself so allusively and obscurely. Vincent Taylor rightly points out that twenty years later the Fourth Evangelist appears to presuppose a polemic, and there is nothing to exclude the possibility that it is implied by the reference to 'divers and strange doctrines' in xiii. 9. He further maintains that if the author, while recognizing the place of the Eucharist in the corporate worship of the Church (but not as a partisan and certainly not as 'a sacramental mystic'), was opposing what he believed to be crude teaching, the language which he uses is precisely what we might expect.

W. Manson rejects both Westcott's and Moffatt's theories, asserting that the passage gives us no positive indication that the writer has the Christian sacrament of communion in mind in this context. In a most unconvincing note Manson seeks a synthesis between the strictures of the writer of Hebrews, his insistence on the difference between the sacrifice offered by Christ and the ordinary sacrifices offered on Jewish altars, and the reality of the meaning which the Church attaches to the use of the observance of the eucharistic service. His identification of 'altar' with the 'upper room' and not Golgotha is not only unfortunate but misleading; for although by 'upper room' he means the institution of the Lord's Supper, he is in fact relating it to Hebrews xiii. 10, and the altar of the upper room becomes identified with *we have an altar*, and in this case the reference would clearly be to the Eucharist which Manson apparently denies.

Many other commentators, far from seeing a difference between the Christian and Jewish sacrifices, observe a parallel between Jewish type and Christian substance. *Tabernacle* must be taken not in a literal, but figurative, sense, and *they* . . . *which serve the tabernacle* are simply 'the worshippers of the sanctuary'. According to Creed, 'The altar of Christian worship is not an altar from which the worshippers of the sanctuary have a right to eat, but an altar which provides cleansing for the heart and conscience.'

In xiii. 9 the author warns them against those who at that time were insisting that reliance upon external ordinances, especially the partaking of meats, was necessary for salvation, rather than reliance upon God's grace alone. These outward observances brought no spiritual profit to those who served the tabernacle. He then in verse 10 adopts Old Testament language in asserting that Christians have an 'altar', but points out that the Jewish people, who acknowledged the sacrifices of the brazen altar and the ritual on atonement day, had no right to eat from it. Reference is then made to Leviticus xvi. 27 to show that the bodies of bullock and goat, which had been sacrificed on the altar, were not eaten by the priests, though they experienced the benefits of the offerings, but were taken and burnt outside the camp. So our Lord, being the antitype of Aaron the high priest, and also the antitype of the expiatory sacrifices, was taken to the altar outside the camp, i.e. the cross, and there offered Himself as the one great sin-offering. As the material bodies of the victims were not eaten outside the camp, so Christ's material body is not eaten; but Christians can partake of the spiritual blessings of the new covenant.

c. Concluding exhortations and benedictions (xiii. 18–25)

18, 19. The author now seeks the intercession of the readers on his behalf. The *us* and the *we* are instances of the 'epistolary plural' as is made clear by the use of the singular in verse 19. It is not necessary, therefore, to think of the *us* as including the leaders, or the companions of the author's labours, or Timothy, as some have suggested. Two considerations are advanced to support his request. First there is the purity of his life and conduct; the very fact that such a statement was necessary suggests that some doubt of this existed in the minds of the readers. Secondly he mentions his desire to revisit them; this suggests that at some former period the author had visited the readers and was known to them. *Restored* does not mean that at the time of writing the author was a prisoner, for according to verse 23 he was at liberty. No reason is given why he was detained, but there appears to have been some obstacle in the way; he believed that through their prayers this could be removed.

20, 21. The AV seems to suggest that the author does not close with a prayer addressed to God but with a benediction addressed to the readers; but the use of the optative *katartisai, perfect*, supports the translation 'now may the God of peace' (RSV). The connection of the title *the God of peace* with the resurrection of Christ suggests 'the God who secures peace for His people through victory over evil'. Yet in view of the trials outside the Church which had created doubts about the new revelation in Christ, and of the conflict within the Church over the authority of the leaders, and of the questioning of the intentions of the author, the translation 'the God who produces (or creates) peace' is better. The God of peace would equip them to do His will *in every good work.*

215

Frequent references have been made in the Epistle to the ascension and glorification of Christ, but *brought again from the dead* is the only direct allusion to His resurrection. The fact that Christ was raised by God in virtue of the eternal covenant is proof that His redeeming work had been accepted and that salvation for His people is assured. In other words, all that is said about Christ in this Epistle is genuine, for God has set His seal upon it. The phrase itself may be reminiscent of Isaiah lxiii. 11, which refers to the bringing up of Moses, the shepherd of the sheep, out of the sea, which, Westcott suggests, 'was a shadow of Christ's ascent from the grave'. The Lord Jesus became the one and only great Shepherd of the sheep in virtue of His shed blood by which the eternal covenant was sealed. He had performed an act which could be repeated by no other, and He received a position which could be held by no other.

The word *katartisai*, translated *make you perfect*, could be used for the reconciliation of factions, or the repairing of broken bones. Its fundamental meaning is 'repairing what is broken' or 'restoring what is lost'. According to Westcott, it 'includes the thoughts of the harmonious combination of different powers (Eph. iv. 12), of the supply of what is defective (1 Thes. iii. 10), and of the amendment of that which is faulty'. If this threefold definition could legitimately be applied to the word in this verse, then in a single word the author provides the solution to all the problems within the Church. The prayer is that all the members may be equipped with all the necessary means which will enable them to do God's will. The will of God for them at that time was to go forth to Jesus outside the camp. They were to make a definite break with Jewish tradition and Jewish nationalism.

22. The tone and severity of the Epistle is softened by the courteous request *suffer* ('bear with', RV), *the word of exhortation,* i.e. give it a friendly reception into your hearts. The high and lofty themes, which run through the Epistle and are so difficult to interpret because of their condensation, rather suggest a profound theological treatise than *a word of exhortation*. Yet Davidson in his introduction reminds us that 'the key-note of the Epistle is struck and heard throughout in the hortatory parts, to which the doctrinal elements are subservient'.

Some commentators find it difficult to believe that the author refers to the whole of these thirteen chapters as a short letter, but they differ considerably as to the part of the Epistle to which *the word of exhortation* refers. Some relate it to the admonitions scattered throughout the letter; others confine it to chapter xiii, and Knox to xiii. 18–25. Yet the use of *epesteila, I have written a letter*, seems to prove that the whole Epistle is meant. Because of the brevity of the Epistle, which could be read aloud in less than an hour, and the vastness of the subject dealt with, the readers are asked to have patience.

23. The author is not trying to confirm what the readers already know, but to impart some new knowledge; therefore the imperative *know ye* is more correct than the indicative 'ye know'. The information is that *our brother Timothy is set at liberty*, i.e. he had been released from prison (cf. Acts iii. 13, iv. 21 where the same Greek word is used). And he promises that if Timothy's arrival is not delayed too long, he will bring Timothy with him when he visits them.

24, 25. To the personal salutation of the author are added in conclusion greetings from some Italian Christians, to all the spiritual leaders and saints. *They of Italy (hoi apo Italias)* can mean either 'residents in Italy', in which case the author is also in Italy and is writing to a Church outside Italy; or it can mean 'those who belong to Italy but who are for the time being resident outside Italy'. If this latter interpretation is correct then the author is outside Italy and writing to Christians in Italy. The phrase, therefore, gives no clue whatever to the place from which, or the persons to whom, the Epistle was written.